Performance
Management

Good luck!

[signature]

Performance Management

Monitoring Teaching in the Primary School

Sara Bubb and
Pauline Hoare

David Fulton Publishers
London

David Fulton Publishers Ltd
Ormond House, 26–27 Boswell Street, London WC1N 3JZ

www.fultonpublishers.co.uk

First published in Great Britain by David Fulton Publishers 2001

British Library Cataloguing in Publication Data
A catalogue record for this book is available from the British Library.

ISBN 1-85346-740-5

The publishers would like to thank John Cox for copy-editing and Priscilla Sharland for proofreading this book

Typeset by Textype Typesetters, Cambridge
Printed in Great Britain by Bell and Bain Ltd, Glasgow

Contents

Preface

Teachers have been subject to unceasing initiatives and an ever-expanding workload. Many initiatives promise to be the one that will really make a difference. Some are potentially very helpful, the trouble is that they are piled on top of each other like the clothes in a jumble sale. Is the Prada original really lurking under that pile of baggy, rumpled unappetising nylon and acrylic cast offs?

Well, we think performance management has the potential to be the Prada of recent initiatives. What is needed is some careful thinking about duplication of effort. Teachers certainly don't have the time to do this. The days of reflective evaluation are long gone: if those secondments really materialise, then perhaps we can use our own resources as a profession to join the debate through the General Teaching Council, through our LEAs and through school networks. But just at the moment we're a bit busy . . . Hence this book. Let us explain.

The core message is that most of the government initiatives are about raising the quality of teaching and learning in our schools: and that's something that teachers have always wanted to do. It's why we joined the profession in the first place after all, because we enjoy learning and we want to pass on that joy to someone else. To teach effectively you need to reflect (and yes, the time for that has evaporated). So the message of this book is that there are ways you can use performance management to capture time to reflect alone and with senior colleagues about what you want to do to make your teaching better. Essentially schools are being given an initiative that will be useful if it is approached in the right way, an initiative that can be harnessed to develop everyone's own continuing professional development.

This book can be used by head teachers as a reflective tool, for school self-review. It can be used by governors to give them an idea of what might be the right kind of questions to be asking in their school. But most of all it is for team leaders and teachers, to show them how they can make a bit more sense of some of the latest initiatives and use them as a vehicle for achieving something that they want: finding out how to be a better teacher.

Sara Bubb and Pauline Hoare
London
March 2001

Reference documents

The following reference documents are available from the standards website (www.standards.dfee.gov.uk)

- Teachers: meeting the challenge of change
- Teachers: meeting the challenge of change – technical consultation document on pay and performance management
- Reviewing Performance of Pay of Heads and Deputy Heads
- Performance Management Framework for Teachers
- Model Performance Management Policy
- Performance Management Guidance Notes
- OFSTED Handbook and Framework for the Inspection of Schools Document.

Acknowledgements

We would like to thank all the peopole who talked through ideas and shared their knowledge and practice with us.

Our past and present PGCE students at the Institute of Education must also be acknowledged, because they have given us such insights into how people learn to be teachers. We hope this book will help them get a fair deal in their first year of teaching and beyond.

Thanks too to Nina Stibbe and all at David Fulton Publishers.

Most of all, we must thank Paul, Julian, Miranda and Oliver; Steve, Lizzie and Rose for their encouragement and tolerance while we wrote this book.

1 Performance management – an overview

The nature of teaching

Teaching is an isolating profession, especially in the primary sector and until recently it was possible to spend one's whole career in the classroom yet never be observed teaching. The good old days some might say, but the downside of this is the lack of recognition and the lack of development. Consider the nursery teacher, 25 years in the classroom, who broke down in tears when she was – finally – told that she was an excellent teacher, with a stunning range of classroom skills. Being told that what you are doing is worthwhile can be validating and empowering. Equally, insensitive handling of situations where teachers need to change or develop their skills can be devastating. A new job in a new school, children from a different type of catchment area, different behavioural and academic expectations can challenge even very confident and experienced teachers: they may need to develop aspects of their professional expertise which they have not used before. Equally, the problem may lie in leadership and management skills at a level above the class teacher. Does the subject coordinator have the appropriate leadership skills to secure improvement in the subject? Does the senior management team have a sure grasp of the issues at a strategic level, so that resources are targeted correctly. Teachers need to be very aware of these potential tensions and associated sensitivities. Used intelligently and creatively, performance management can be the key which unlocks these difficult situations.

The reasons for performance management

Performance management was introduced from September 2000 and is effectively the successor to appraisal. The appraisal system was adopted in many schools, but not all. Even where appraisal has, for a variety of reasons, fallen into disuse, very many schools regularly carry out professional interviews, with the purpose of linking school and individual needs. Where the appraisal system was adopted, schools have found it helpful in linking the needs of the school as expressed through the school development plan with the aspirations of teachers in terms of their own professional development. The purpose of performance management is to strengthen these strands, so that the professional development of teachers and therefore also their pleasure and satisfaction with the profession of teaching is increasingly linked with the progress of pupils and the success of the school.

1

In some quarters, performance management is regarded solely as a system adapted from the business world with the intention of helping schools improve the service they give to their pupils. It is true that many aspects of performance management have been adapted from aspects of business practice, but this view ignores the prior work done in many schools through the appraisal system. The Green Paper (DfEE 1998d) was the development of a new avenue, intended to lead to improved accountability, higher standards and greater success for pupils. It was predicated on a fusion between the best that had so far been achieved by leading schools and best practice in business.

The place of performance management in school

Performance management is firmly linked to threshold assessment, and that in turn links to the new standards that were introduced for aspiring head teachers through the National Professional Qualifications for Headships (NPQH), for serving head teachers, and for newly qualified teachers (NQTs) under the induction standards. It is designed to support school improvement and the raising of standards. It is part of a range of measures introduced over the last few years. The National Literacy and Numeracy Strategies were originally put in place with the intention of eventually ensuring that all 16-year-olds leave school with a basic competence in reading and writing. Teachers have implemented these strategies and have achieved much success (OFSTED 2000a) but this concentration on core skills has revealed areas where schools need to target their efforts more closely to the needs of the pupils they serve. For example, the underachievement of boys in writing (OFSTED 1999a) and of ethnic minorities, in particular black Afro-Caribbean groups (OFSTED 2000a, b, and particularly d). This is the background to the widening of the school improvement agenda through performance management, threshold assessment and external advice to governing bodies.

From September 2000 schools had to put in place a new performance management system which includes:

- agreeing annual objectives for each teacher, including objectives relating to pupil progress and ways of developing and improving teachers' professional practice;
- for head teachers, objectives relating to school leadership and management and pupil progress;
- in-year monitoring of progress and classroom observation of teachers;
- an end of year review meeting, which involves an assessment of teachers' overall performance, taking account of achievement against objectives, agreeing objectives for the coming year and discussion of professional development opportunities/activities;
- using performance review outcomes to inform pay decisions, where appropriate.

Teachers are often resentful of businessmen and women demanding closer attention to basic skills, but fundamentally it is the success of the national economy that pays teachers' wages. World markets are very difficult to access if a quarter of your workforce can hardly read or work out change from 50p, let alone operate a computer effectively. The questions that people in government and industry are asking can be boiled down to one: 'Why can't young people who've spent 11 years in compulsory education read and write?' This question has been asked since the 1970s, and more recently, shortly before OFSTED was set up in 1993. At this point, 40 per cent of school leavers in the UK, as against 70 per cent in Germany, and more than 80 per cent in Japan left school with a craft/technician diploma or above (Brighouse and Moon 1995). Many different theories have been put forward for these low levels of qualification after 11 years of compulsory education: trendy teaching methods; government legislation undermining the structure of the family; the continual change forced on schools; the collapse of religion – the list varies according to political allegiances. Whatever the causes, such a high level of illiteracy needs addressing. Performance management is in many ways the next layer of the campaign for increasing the levels of literacy and numeracy.

The purpose of performance management

Performance management is a system for reviewing and agreeing priorities within the context of the school development plan. Its purposes can be characterised in a range of ways. It may be described as a pyramidal hierarchy of objectives: for the institution, for the management and for the teachers. In this sense it is the institutional mirror image of target setting for pupils. Its objective is to improve the match between the offered and the received curriculum. The way it sets about this is by encouraging schools to support teachers' work as individuals and in teams through the process of setting, agreeing and reviewing school objectives. There are links to the discretionary pay awards that governing bodies make: how the governors decide to do this is a matter for debate in each governing body. To dismiss the process as 'performance related pay' (PRP) and then to state that 'It didn't work in industry' is inaccurate. As a system it is far more sophisticated than approaches used in industry (ACAS 1990, Ironside and Siefert 1995, Sisson 1995.)

System linkages with performance management

Between 1999 and 2000 the DfEE spent £7.296 billion on primary schools and £9.037 billion on secondary schools. It is fair to ask whether the government is getting value for money on behalf of the taxpayers. It is also fair for the government to establish systems for finding out how effectively schools spend the huge national investment that has been delegated to them. Performance management was introduced after national consultation as an equitable way of raising standards and rewarding teachers who contribute effectively to the efforts of the school as a whole to drive forward pupil progress. The system works by encouraging schools to support teachers as individuals and in teams through the process of setting, agreeing and reviewing school objectives.

The newness of the system has antagonised many teachers. The victims of constant change for more than ten years, it is not surprising that in some quarters there is a distinct lack of enthusiasm for yet another initiative. However, recent publications like *Recognising Progress – Getting the most from your data* (DfEE 2000c), provide a useful explanation of how performance management links directly to the production of the school development plan, supports the collection of data for threshold assessment and can be used as an effective method for raising standards.

Data analysis

During the collection of data for the threshold process, teachers raised concerns about the validity of statistical data. It should always be borne in mind that statistics can be used to support or oppose any argument: they are a device for working out what questions to ask. This is the area where most teachers' skills are at their weakest. Statistics do not normally form part of an arts degree, although the psychology and social sciences graduates will have had some training in the use and interpretation of statistics as part of their first degree (Beresford 1999). National agencies accept test data as a starting point. It should not be regarded as a final judgement on the worth of schools or of teachers, although this is how many teachers perceive it. Representatives of government and non-governmental organisations (NGO) are attempting to find out via such statistics how to address levels of illiteracy and innumeracy. Statistics are a way of discovering what questions it may be useful to ask, they should not be regarded as an answer in themselves. The picture presented through statistics gives a very partial picture of the strengths and achievements of different schools.

In the world of statistics, it is possible to predict the theoretical gain that a child might make in each term at school, and measure how far in advance or how far behind the expected rate of progress that particular pupil is.

To gain a full picture of the school's overall performance, it is useful to consider the performance of the complete year cohort. For example, you could consider the attainment of boys, ethnic minorities and English as Additional Language (EAL) pupils against progress made nationally, and the impact this has on the school's overall performance. By looking at the performance of different groups of pupils in this way, you can get a more complete picture of the school's overall performance, and this will help you with the setting of challenging yet realistic targets.

When analysing your school's performance, it is helpful to probe for reasons why pupils have made better or worse progress than expected. The questions listed are useful for identifying priorities and strategies for school improvement.

Some questions for you to consider include:

- How does the progress made by pupils in different groups, sets or classes compare? Are there any noticeable differences in the progress made by boys, girls and ethnic minorities in each class?
- Have any pupils made unexpectedly good progress, or significantly less progress than expected? Are there any marked differences and if so can the teacher or the pupils, think of any reasons?
- In classes or groups where the majority of pupils make better than average progress, can teachers identify any teaching practices that they think contribute to their success? From the comparisons and discussions, what are the emerging priorities for the school?
- How do teachers set their expectations of pupils at the beginning of Years 1 and 2? Do pupils with high or low prior attainment make the progress expected of them?
- How do parents' and pupils' expectations of future performance compare with the information shown in the Progress Charts?

> - If parents' and pupils' own expectations are low, can they identify any particular aspects of work they find difficult and where they would benefit from extra help?
> - How do teachers' forecasts and expectations for their pupils compare to what the Progress Charts suggest they could achieve? What are the reasons behind any low teacher expectations – what needs to be done, in the classroom or in other ways, to counter low expectations?

© Bubb and Hoare 2001

In the real world, where divorce, homelessness and all the other myriad horrors that beset children come into play, such notional progress may be impossible. The real story is of course, infinitely complex. It is part of the job of the school management to develop awareness among teachers that there are demanding, measurable expectations expressed through performance management, but at the same time emphasise the human side also. Teachers need to be fully aware of the demands and expectations coming from government and the local education authority and also to understand the shortcomings of the data. They need to be aware that the notional progress expected must be viewed in relation to the personal, social and emotional context of the individual child. In other words a holistic view is needed – plus a healthy degree of realism.

Monitoring

As well as rigorous data analysis, performance management also requires regular monitoring. Pupil achievement may vary over a year for a wide variety of reasons, and it is not acceptable to wait for the end of year results before realising that there has been a problem of some kind. This is why pupil progress will always form at least one of the objectives set for the head teacher's own performance management interview. In most cases this will be linked to some form of report to the governing body that requires both data analysis and the monitoring of teaching. It is also likely that monitoring will also form an important part of the objectives set for senior teachers and members of the senior management team. This aspect of continuous monitoring is one of the major areas where performance management differs from business PRP systems. Continuous monitoring of how the development plan is working is difficult to arrange in a business environment. In a school, however, the main business is teaching and learning, with the aim of raising standards. Teachers are very familiar with target setting, and the layered target setting that has been an integral part of the Literacy Strategy for the last 18 months means that teachers who are eligible to cross the threshold will be very aware of exactly how they will be getting the three points progress required. They will be very conscious of the school targets submitted to the DfEE through the LEA, and will probably have participated in the school-based process of agreeing those targets. They will also be very aware of their key stage targets and how these translate into year group targets. Good teachers will be using the guidance offered through the Literacy Strategy to set targets for different groups, and at an individual level for pupils of unusually high ability through IAPs (individual achievement plans) and for those with special educational needs through IEPs (individual education plans).

Contextual analysis

Performance management demands that firstly the school considers and analyses the context and the content of statutory assessment. During this process, the school will record and analyse SATs results, non-statutory test results, and other in-school assessment systems (detailed in Chapter 4). It is necessary to carry out an evaluation of how different groups perform: are girls outperforming boys? Why? Is the way that reading is presented encouraging to boys? Is the range of non-fiction sufficiently wide and interesting to encourage their reading development? What stimuli are offered during creative writing? Are these equally accessible to either gender? The questions that result from an analysis of the data are many, and will be equally challenging as the data is analysed in terms of ethnic group or in terms of educational needs. This type of analysis, and more importantly the sets of questions it provokes are of key importance in helping the teachers to see how the school can use this data to plan for the future. In most primary schools, the head and deputy will be the people most closely involved in the interpretation of test results. The challenges for the future are to involve a wider audience, consisting not just of the teaching staff, but also governors and parents.

Performance management is a framework within which schools can examine what they are doing and check how effective it is. It also provides a system for developing new initiatives where necessary. There is a wide range of good practice in schools, and another challenge for the future is how to share this richness of experience across a range of schools.

Investors in People in schools

Some schools are investing time and effort in working towards Investors in People (IiP) status. Currently around 7 per cent of schools are recognised as Investors in People, with a higher percentage of schools in the secondary sector involved than in the primary sector. An interesting correlation has emerged between OFSTED reports and the achievement of Investors in People status. The research (Kendall *et al.* 2000) indicates that schools with Investors in People accreditation and also schools working towards accreditation receive higher assessments of teaching quality than schools that do not use the standard. There are also very marked links between IiP and performance management. The major difference is that IiP applies to all staff, and performance management applies only to teaching staff.

Change has become a way of life for everyone, not just schools. The pace of change may vary from time to time, but it is highly unlikely that it will abate, and pressures on leadership in particular are likely to intensify in the future. This is essentially why the DfEE has moved to introduce performance management: it provides a set of levers with which to change processes and practices within the school. The IiP standards are essentially a more sophisticated version: the Rolls Royce of school improvement for instance. The major resource of any school is its staff, *all* its staff, and school improvement cannot be achieved without the development of the staff. It is a most effective way of making sure that the school is a 'learning organisation', and one which promotes lifelong learning for both staff and pupils.

6

The purpose of IiP is to illustrate how different initiatives and different improvements can form a more effective coherent whole. Schools often feel that they are struggling in a morass of paperwork made up of a thousand different initiatives. IiP provides a context and a framework for this apparent confusion and enables the head teacher to lead the school through this, using initiatives positively and effectively for the benefit of the school. Support for senior managers is provided by:

- recognising that enhanced pupil achievement lies at the heart of school improvement;
- linking with other national standards and frameworks;
- promoting partnership with all involved in supporting the school;
- nurturing the school as a learning organisation;
- contributing to the development of school ethos and culture;
- promoting the value of continuing professional development;
- focusing on the impact of training and development.

The NFER research (Kendall *et al.* 2000) also showed that schools engaged in the IiP process found that staff were more willing to accept criticism, and that there was a greater questioning of processes and practices within the school. The greatest beneficiaries of IiP were felt to be support staff, who typically became more involved in planning, had more opportunities for professional development and felt more valued within the school.

The accompanying three charts clearly show the powerful nature of the IiP process and its strong links with school improvement through the raising of standards.

The role of the head teacher

The role of the head teacher has changed out of all recognition over the last ten years. That role may still be defined as 'the leading professional', but the general understanding of what heads should do has altered drastically. The rapid pace of change has meant that even relatively new head teachers feel that their own class teaching skills are quickly out of date, and for those with many years successful headship behind them, a practical knowledge of managing a class in the face of the demands of the National Curriculum may be an unlearnt skill. However, many in education confuse the skills required for headship with those required for teaching. Effective skills at this level are still not fully understood: the resonances between leadership and followership have not been fully investigated. Furthermore, there is a great deal of confusion about how the skills of an effective head teacher grow out of the skills learnt in the classroom. Do head teachers need to teach regularly? If they enjoy it certainly, if it is too time-consuming then it should only be considered if there is an emergency or if it is necessary to demonstrate particular lessons to staff. The real skills of the head teacher lie elsewhere.

Consider the arts: an appreciation of music or painting requires knowledge of the context from which the work of art has sprung, but does not require a technical mastery equal to that of the artist or performer. Similarly a head teacher may bring experience and insight to the process of teaching, based on broad experience. This experience may be effectively communicated via observation as well as through

Linking the Standard to Key Issues and Processes

Key issues for schools	How Investors in People helps	Links to: OFSTED Framework, NPQH, DfEE Performance Management procedures
Raising pupil achievement	• encourages sharing models of good practice • requires that goals and targets for pupil achievement are clear and focused • links development of people to the school's goals and targets	**OFSTED:** What progress do pupils make and how does this compare with similar schools? Raising achievement through teaching and learning **NPQH:** Teachers' objectives relating to pupil progress **Performance Management:**
Ensuring effective leadership and management	• promotes the clarification of roles and responsibilities • provides a framework for managing change with staff support • promotes targeted monitoring and evaluation integrates people development with school improvement planning	**OFSTED:** How well is the school led and managed? **NPQH:** Strategic direction and development of the school **Performance Management:** Headteacher objectives for leadership and management
Promoting the achievement of individual staff	• ensures that staff development practices are related to goals and targets • promotes staff responsibility for their own learning and that of others	**OFSTED:** How well are pupils taught? **NPQH:** Leading and managing staff **Performance Management:** Annual review for teachers includes pupils progress and professional development objectives
Using national data, benchmarks and standards	• supports the capacity of schools to focus on performance outcomes • promotes confidence with benchmarking and the rigorous review of performance targets • is itself a national standard	**OFSTED:** How high are standards? **NPQH:** Core purpose of headteacher and key outcomes of headship **Performance Management:** School targets and head/deputy objectives
Promoting social inclusion and equity	• encourages flexible planning to focus on individual potential • promotes the development of staff skills and attitudes to meet new demands • requires commitment to equality of opportunity in the development of people	**OFSTED:** How good are the curricular and other opportunities for pupils? **NPQH:** Core purpose of headteacher includes ensuring equality of opportunity for all. Headteachers to show they are meeting needs of all pupils **Performance Management:** Equity an underlying principle of effective performance management
Promoting values for life	• supports the development of the desired vision and culture • emphasises the crucial importance of effective communication • recognises the importance of lifelong learning and development for all	**OFSTED:** How well does the school work in partnership with parents? How well does the school care for its pupils? **NPQH:** Included in key outcomes of headship **Performance Management:** Promoting lifelong learning
Continuous improvement	• promotes the value of people continuing to develop, in order to sustain overall performance improvement • enhances monitoring, evaluation and review of pupil outcomes to promote improved performance	**OFSTED:** School self-review and monitoring procedures **NPQH:** Continuous improvement in quality of education part of core purpose of headteacher **Performance Management:** Annual review of headteacher/deputy/teacher targets/objectives
Managing resources	• encourages identification of the true costs and benefits of developing people • requires targeting of staff development resources to meet identified goals • encourages schools to compare, challenge, consult and compete for Best Value	**OFSTED:** Efficiency and Value for Money **NPQH:** Strategic management of staff and resources **Performance Management:** Promotes provision of effective and efficient staff development activity

The chart shows in summary form the links between key issues faced by schools, the Investors in People Standard, the OFSTED Framework for Inspection and NPQH.

School Improvement Cycle	Performance Management Cycle

School Improvement Cycle

AUTUMN TERM
1 **How well are we doing?**
2 **How do we compare with similar schools?**

Team/Subject Leaders
- Analysing/interpretation trends in whole school data
- Sharing outcomes of analysis with staff

Class Teachers
- Participating in discussion of whole school performance data

3 **What more should we aim to achieve?**
Team Leaders
- Co-ordinating individual end of key stage target setting
- Arriving at whole school end of key stage targets each year from individual end of key stage targets and from analysis of whole school performance data
- Agreeing statutory targets with Governing Body

Subject Leaders
- Participating in individual end of key stage target setting for subject area
- Arriving at whole school targets for subject area each year from individual end of key stage targets and from analysis of whole school performance data (in conjunction with management team and class teachers)

Class Teachers
- Participating in end of key stage target setting.

4 **What must we do to make it happen?**
Team/Subject Leaders
- Reviewing/amending long term curriculum plans and School Improvement/Development Plan to support progress towards end of key stage targets
- Implementing Performance Management Cycle across school

Class Teachers
- Participating in reviewing long term plans and School Improvement Plan

THROUGHOUT YEAR/SUMMER TERM
5 **Taking action and reviewing progress**
Team/Subject Leaders
- Monitoring progress of year groups towards end of year pupil progress objectives (Performance Management Cycle) and towards end of key stage targets (School Improvement Cycle)

Performance Management Cycle

AUTUMN TERM
Agreeing objectives
Team Leaders
- Identifying pupil progress objectives (end of year targets) with individual staff for each class:
- Agreeing professional development objectives with individual staff.

Class Teachers
- Identifying pupil progress objectives (end of year targets) for their classes;
- Identifying professional development objectives for coming year.

Agreeing a work and development plan
Team/Subject Leaders
- Agreeing medium term plans with each teacher to support progress of each year group towards their pupil progress objectives (end of year targets)
- Agreeing plans to achieve professional development objectives with each teacher

Class Teachers
- Identifying learning objectives in medium term plans that reflect progress towards pupil progress objectives
- Reviewing/amending medium term planning to support progress towards pupil progress objectives
- Agreeing plans to achieve professional development objectives

THROUGHOUT YEAR
Teaching and Learning – Monitoring Progress in Year
Team/Subject Leaders
- Monitoring progress of year groups against pupil progress objectives and progress of staff against professional development objectives

Class Teachers
- Identifying short term learning objectives from medium term plans and from strategies as basis for on-going teaching;
- Using assessment information from on-going teaching to monitor progress towards learning objectives in medium term plans;
- Adjusting teaching in the light of this monitoring.

SUMMER TERM
End of year review of progress
Team Leaders
- Reviewing progress towards pupil progress objectives and professional development objectives with each teacher

Class Teachers
- Reviewing progress towards pupil progress objectives and professional development objectives, identifying issues that may need to be addressed in the coming year.

direct teaching. In some cases, a viewer or listener may be better placed than the artist to offer comment: an experienced listener may be in a position to offer a fresh viewpoint based on a wider listening to the classical repertoire for instance that might provide valuable insights for a virtuoso but inexperienced performer. In the same way, an experienced head teacher or senior manager may bring a wide range of experience in different contexts to enrich the work of individual teachers. This may be further enhanced by experience across a range of local authorities. These typically range from the highly effective to the utterly disastrous. A head teacher who has seen, in person, how low educational standards can depress the life chances of a whole generation in a particular area will have an extra determination to ensure that the same thing does not happen in his or her school. He or she will also have a rich fund of practical experience of how head teachers have tackled real problems in other schools. The value of this approach is borne out by the research paper produced by OFSTED (1993) on the inspection system currently used in South Australia, which relies heavily on the expertise of serving head teachers and experienced teachers whose motivation lies in the extending of their own personal experience as a result of the period of secondment involved.

Thus, in terms of headship, we are talking about a wide knowledge of teaching, not confined to one specific school or authority, the ability to evaluate problems as a result of this wide knowledge, combined with powers of synthesis, explanation and persuasion to lead the staff in the direction that will result in progress. One important part of this range of skills is the ability to monitor the quality of teaching accurately, sympathetically and helpfully. It is at this point that the difference between an OFSTED inspector and a head teacher becomes apparent. The inspector must operate his or her judgement impartially and ruthlessly in the interests of the children in any particular school. The head teacher must have an equal facility and skill but profoundly more developed sensitivities: he or she sails a J class yacht in the Southern Ocean. When is the right moment to crowd on all the sail? When is the time to strip the masts, batten down the hatches and run before the storm, hoping to make up time later? It is the evaluative faculty linked to sensitivity for people that creates the successful school.

Yet the head teacher must always be aware of the whole picture and also the myriad component parts. The perspective of what is happening in other parts of the school is a key area for comparison. Techniques used by one teacher in a particular class may be particularly effective, but unless there is a mechanism for sharing and disseminating such good practice, it will not be available to all pupils. Clearly this includes aspects of equal opportunities, making sure that all pupils irrespective of gender, ethnic origin or disability receive the best that the school has to offer. It is in this sense that monitoring has become an increasingly important part of the repertoire of the head teacher and the senior management team.

A key responsibility for head teachers is monitoring. Irrespective of the requirements for performance management, it is a necessity for equal opportunities. Head teachers need a fine-tuned awareness of what is good about their schools and what needs to be improved. They find this out through monitoring teachers in the classroom. They look at teachers teaching, and the outcomes; they look at teachers' preparation by looking at the long-term, mid-term and short-term planning for the class and different curriculum subjects. The task of keeping a finger on the pulse soon becomes so large as to become unmanageable, and it requires careful judgement to decide when it needs to be delegated to curriculum coordinators and members of the senior management team. Many other areas beyond subjects need to be observed: behaviour and work rate for example. An equally onerous task is the compilation and monitoring of work samples.

The roles of a team leader

The structure of the middle management in a primary school will vary according to the philosophy of the school and its size. Some schools operate a subject coordinator system, others, a year group leader structure; some even combine the two by having subject coordinators and key stage leaders. However the middle management is structured, the role is a vital one. The team leader explains the rationale of the school's plans and policies to the class teacher and is instrumental in securing their understanding and agreement. They are responsible for observing, setting and reviewing objectives with the class teachers. It is very much a role of dialogue: the engagement in professional debate and discussion is what secures the full-hearted cooperation of teachers in initiatives like performance management. One of the shortcomings of the system as it stands is that this level has little or no overt training. The system relies on the professionalism of the team leader to secure their own professional development.

The team leader is the person with specific responsibility for a teacher. It is a really important role and one which is very rewarding. Some have said that it is their favourite of all their roles within the school. One way of thinking about the sort of team leader you would like to be is to analyse what it was that the people that have helped you be a better teacher did or said. The significant colleagues in our careers engaged with us at a high level in thinking about education. They were people who held the same educational philosophy as us, and had the same values. We shared many interests and sense of humour. They believed in us – and that gave us confidence to try new things.

The role of the classroom teacher

The essential problem with monitoring is that teaching and learning are part of a time-dependent process. It really is not possible for an observer to gain a full and true knowledge of another teacher's work through a single observation. Teachers are professionals and the drive for monitoring should include much emphasis on the individual's continuing professional development. Teachers enjoy teaching. They go through a long and arduous training, undergo some financial hardship and at the end of the process they receive only a moderate financial reward, when judged by the general level of wage awards in the private sector. They are teachers because they are committed to the idea of educating children, because they want to impart their own knowledge and because they want to improve children's life chances.

Given that this is so, any monitoring programme must also provide for individual teachers' continuing professional development. Ways of doing this might be through a regular programme of release, focused on a school priority such as assessment, with each teacher given a fair share of time in colleagues' classrooms (QCA 1999). Visits to other schools are the natural extension to this. This approach reduces the anxiety levels of teachers because they should be convinced that the process of observation and monitoring is about teaching and learning; that it is a two-way process, where the observer may be learning and making evaluations simultaneously. It also reduces the idea that there is a punitive aspect to monitoring: if everyone is participating in the process, it immediately becomes palpably fairer.

However, time is always at a premium. Schools also need to consider how to use video in an appropriate way to promote professional development. Given that the basic teaching qualifications are set by DfEE Circular 4/98 (DfEE 1998b), teachers early in their careers will find that much of the extensive Teacher Training Agency (TTA) material will be useful (TTA 2000). The videos provide extensive teaching extracts, supported by examples of the teacher's planning and assessment. The materials can be used very effectively to support teachers who have qualified, but have yet to meet the threshold criteria. Schools can use extracts from a particular unit to support individual teachers, or teachers who wish to develop an aspect of their professional expertise can focus on particular areas of the text and video.

The materials provide a range of examples related to all the standards required for qualified teacher status (QTS). For example, the following extract from DfEE 4/98 shows the complexity of what is expected of those aspiring to be teachers:

B4: Planning
(a) plan their teaching to achieve progression in pupils' learning through:

  (iv) setting clear targets for pupils' learning, building on prior attainment, and ensuring that pupils are aware of the substance and purpose of what they are asked to do;

(b) make effective use of assessment information on pupils' attainment and progress in their teaching and in planning future lessons and sequences of lessons.

These criteria are equally valid for teachers early in their careers and also for those teachers who have not had appropriate ongoing professional training during the recent and far-reaching changes in the educational world. Individual teachers who aspire to cross the threshold over the next few years, and schools who want to provide support for teachers should consider using the TTA materials as part of a programme encouraging staff to reflect on strengths and weaknesses in teaching.

The teacher has always had to assess children to see how much they have learned. It is now the head's responsibility to collect assessment information. Test results compare the performance of each successive cohort within a school and offer a rain check on whether standards are rising, declining or being maintained. They can also be used as a benchmark to compare schools. Test results point to learning that should take place by a specified and agreed point in the future.

The role of the governing body

The role of the governing body is, as always, to see the big picture, and to ask what might seem obvious questions:

How do you know that?
Are we doing as well as we can?
What about schools that are like us?

In the avalanche of paperwork through which schools have to struggle, this view can be obscured. It is vitally important that the system contains some internal checks and balances, so that the professionals do not get carried away with the theory, the latest initiatives and so forth. A responsible governing body which asks the right questions is beyond price.

The management of a school will have had to collect the right data, have analysed it, understood it and so be able to explain it in ordinary language. A governor with responsibility for special educational needs (SEN) or for early years, may carry out a useful role in securing funds or recognition for teachers in these areas as a direct result of, for example, observing good use being made of ICT in the context of SEN, or recommending the direction of funds towards the provision of large outdoor toys for the nursery.

Monitoring includes the perusal of year on year figures for example, so the governors' role clearly includes consideration of annual test results for particular cohorts. It might usefully be extended to developing some familiarity with looking at work samples: useful in the event of turbulence, when the previous year's results may not be capable of comparison with the current data.

Monitoring may also include receiving reports about subjects. Since the roles of the senior management team and the coordinators are to deputise for the head in the process of information gathering and evaluation of findings, every coordinator ought to be able to write a report or give a presentation to a governing body that outlines standards achieved in the subject and what the plans for improving standards might be.

Before starting to monitor teachers it is important to think about what effective teaching is. In the next chapter we shall look at criteria for judging teaching.

2 Criteria for judging teaching

Before one starts monitoring teaching it is important to have a clear understanding of what an effective teacher is. This seems simple but in fact it is the subject of much debate. Teachers who have been in the profession a long time will be aware of the fashion element. At the moment whole-class teaching is very fashionable, but it has not always been so – at times it was absolutely frowned upon.

There are various definitions of the components of effective teaching that look different but which are really just variations of a theme. The ones you need to be aware of are:

– the OFSTED criteria for teaching;
– the standards for qualified teacher status;
– the induction standards;
– the threshold standards;
– the Hay McBer characteristics of effective teachers.

As you read below the different criteria look for the recurring themes, such as subject knowledge and assessment. How does this fit in with your idea of an effective teacher?

The OFSTED criteria for teaching

It is really useful to study the criteria that OFSTED inspectors use (Figure 2.1), thinking about how they relate to your teaching context. Note that both teaching and the children's learning are used to make an overall judgement on teachers' effectiveness.

In determining their judgements, inspectors consider the extent to which teachers:

- show good subject knowledge and understanding in the way they present and discuss their subject;
- are technically competent in teaching phonics and other basic skills;
- plan effectively, setting clear objectives that pupils understand;
- challenge and inspire pupils, expecting the most of them, so as to deepen their knowledge and understanding;
- use methods which enable all pupils to learn effectively;
- manage pupils well and insist on high standards of behaviour;
- use time, support staff and other resources, especially information and communications technology, effectively;
- assess pupils' work thoroughly and use assessments to help and encourage pupils to overcome difficulties;

- use homework effectively to reinforce and/or extend what is learned in school;

and the extent to which pupils:

- acquire new knowledge or skills, develop ideas and increase their understanding;
- apply intellectual, physical or creative effort in their work;
- are productive and work at a good pace;
- show interest in their work, are able to sustain concentration and think and learn for themselves;
- understand what they are doing, how well they have done and how they can improve.

Figure 2.1 The OFSTED criteria for judging teaching

Figure 2.2 The OFSTED criteria for judging teaching – diagram (Hay McBer 2000)

The standards for qualified teacher status

There are about 77 standards (DfEE 1998b) and sub-standards for students wanting to be primary teachers, but an additional 15 for those qualifying to teach reception and nursery classes, making a total of 92. In the Initial Teacher Training National Curricula for English, mathematics, science and ICT there are hundreds of further standards. The QTS standards are organised under the following headings:

A. Knowledge and Understanding
B. Planning, Teaching and Class Management
C. Monitoring, Assessment, Recording, Reporting and Accountability
D. Other Professional Requirements

Each standard is set out discretely for clarity (see Appendix). However, the guidance from the TTA is that they can also be treated as a whole or grouped together. As the TTA states,

> Professionalism implies more than meeting a series of discrete standards. It is necessary to consider the standards as a whole to appreciate the creativity, commitment, energy and enthusiasm which teaching demands, and the intellectual and managerial skills required of the effective professional. (TTA 1999a, p.12)

The standards are very demanding – they describe the best sort of teacher rather than a beginner. Colin Richards (2000), in a letter to the *Times Educational Supplement*, wrote,

> The standards represent an impossible set of demands which properly exemplified would need the omnicompetence of Leonardo da Vinci, the diplomatic expertise of Kofi Annan, the histrionic skills of Julie Walters, the grim determination of Alex Ferguson, and the saintliness of Mother Teresa, coupled with the omniscience of God.

Planning, Teaching and Class Management
(a) sets clear targets for improvement of pupils' achievement, monitors pupils' progress towards those targets and uses appropriate teaching strategies in the light of this, including, where appropriate, in relation to literacy, numeracy and other school targets;

(b) plans effectively to ensure that pupils have the opportunity to meet their potential, notwithstanding differences of race and gender, and taking account of the needs of pupils who are:

- underachieving;
- very able;
- not yet fluent in English;

making use of relevant information and specialist help where available;

(c) secures a good standard of pupil behaviour in the classroom through establishing appropriate rules and high expectations of discipline which pupils respect, acting to pre-empt and deal with inappropriate behaviour in the context of the behaviour policy of the school;

(d) plans effectively, where applicable, to meet the needs of pupils with Special Educational Needs and, in collaboration with the SENCO, makes an appropriate contribution to the preparation, implementation, monitoring and review of Individual Education Plans;

(e) takes account of ethnic and cultural diversity to enrich the curriculum and raise achievement;

Monitoring, Assessment, Recording, Reporting and Accountability
(f) recognises the level that a pupil is achieving and makes accurate assessments, independently, against attainment targets, where applicable, and performance levels associated with other tests or qualifications relevant to the subject(s) or phase(s) taught;

Figure 2.3 The induction standards (DfEE 1999a)

(g) liaises effectively with pupils' parents/carers through informative oral and written reports on pupils' progress and achievements, discussing appropriate targets, and encouraging them to support their children's learning, behaviour and progress;

Other Professional Requirements

(h) where applicable, deploys support staff and other adults effectively in the classroom, involving them, where appropriate, in the planning and management of pupils' learning;

(i) takes responsibility for implementing school policies and practices, including those dealing with bullying and racial harassment;

(j) takes responsibility for their own professional development, setting objectives for improvements, and taking action to keep up-to-date with research and developments in pedagogy and in the subject(s) they teach.

Figure 2.3 *cont.*

Activity 2.1
Analysing the Induction Standards

Focusing on one standard at a time:
Discuss what you think it means. (This will involve unpacking its components.)

What would an NQT need to do to demonstrate that they were doing it:
  Well?
  Passably?
  Unsatisfactorily?

What help would an NQT need if they were not achieving the standard?

Make a list of any issues of debate.

The induction standards

As well as meeting the QTS standards consistently, NQTs must meet the ten induction standards (see Figure 2.3). They are arranged under the same headings as the QTS standards, but there are no further standards for knowledge and understanding.

There are some important issues concerning the induction standards.

- The standards describe a perfect teacher, not someone at the start of their career.
- Each standard is wide reaching.
- All the standards are open to interpretation.
- They are hard to assess. There is no description of what a borderline pass would look like.
- The success of an individual NQT depends largely upon the practice in their school.
- Many of the standards are cutting edge practice – more may be expected of NQTs than others.

Threshold Standards

Knowledge and Understanding
Teachers should demonstrate that they have a thorough and up-to-date knowledge of the teaching of their subject(s) and take account of wider curriculum developments which are relevant to their work.

Teaching and Assessment
Teachers should demonstrate that they consistently and effectively:

- plan lessons and sequences of lessons to meet pupils' individual learning needs
- use a range of appropriate strategies for teaching and classroom management
- use information about prior attainment to set well-grounded expectations for pupils
- monitor progress to give clear and constructive feedback.

Pupil Progress
Teachers should demonstrate that, as a result of their teaching, their pupils achieve well relative to the pupil's prior attainment, making progress as good or better than similar pupils nationally. This should be shown in marks or grades in any relevant national tests or examinations, or school-based assessment for pupils where national tests and examinations are not taken.

Wider Professional Effectiveness
Teachers should demonstrate that they:

- take responsibility for their professional development and use the outcomes to improve their teaching and pupils' learning
- make an active contribution to the policies and aspirations of the school.

Professional Characteristics
Teachers should demonstrate that they are effective professionals who challenge and support all pupils to do their best through:

- inspiring trust and confidence
- building team commitment
- engaging and motivating pupils
- analytical thinking
- positive action to improve the quality of pupils' learning.

Figure 2.4 The threshold standards (DfEE 2000g)

- NQTs must meet all the standards – meeting nine standards very well cannot compensate for not meeting one.

The threshold standards

To pass the threshold, teachers have to have reached spine point 9 of the salary scale and meet the eight threshold standards (Figure 2.4). They cover five areas all of which relate directly or indirectly to classroom teaching.

The Hay McBer (2000) characteristics of effective teachers

The Hay McBer research found three main factors within teachers' control that significantly influence pupil progress: teaching skills, professional characteristics and classroom climate (Figure 2.5). Each provides distinctive and complementary ways that teachers can understand the contribution they make. None can be relied on alone to deliver value-added teaching.

The three factors are different in nature. Two of them – professional characteristics and teaching skills – are factors which relate to what a teacher brings to the job. The professional characteristics are the ongoing patterns of behaviour that combine to drive the things teachers typically do. Among those things are the 'micro-behaviours' covered by teaching skills. While teaching skills can be learned, sustaining these behaviours over the course of a career will depend on the deeper seated nature of professional characteristics. Classroom climate, on the other hand, is an output measure. It allows teachers to understand how the pupils in their class feel and what influences their motivation to learn.

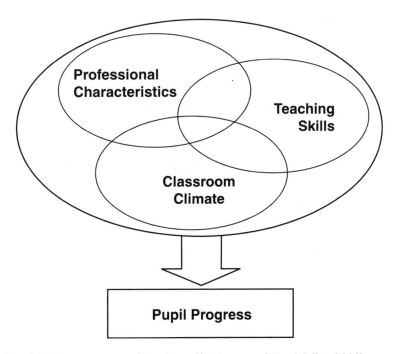

Figure 2.5 Hay McBer measures of teacher effectiveness (Hay McBer 2000)

The following were listed by Hay McBer as professional characteristics.

Professionalism
Challenge and Support
Confidence
Creating Trust
Respect for Others

Thinking
Analytical Thinking
Conceptual Thinking

Planning and Setting Expectations
Drive for Improvement
Information Seeking
Initiative

Leading
Flexibility
Holding People Accountable
Managing Pupils' Passion for Learning

Relating to Others
Impact and Influence
Teamworking
Understanding Others

The 'good enough' teacher

Having looked at five current sets of criteria for teaching we can see an emphasis on itemising components of competence in a mechanistic way. We can also see very high standards set for beginning teachers – ones that experienced teachers have not been required to meet, and which they might struggle with.

Winnacott (1971) once wrote of the 'good enough' mother – a very comforting idea. We all know what we should be – the perfect parent, partner, lover, child, sibling – but no one can be perfect all the time. Let us aim at being good enough – I'm sure we'll all feel happier! The QTS and induction standards in their description of a beginning teacher make us shrivel with inadequacy because we are not sure we would meet them every day, after twenty years in the job! Let us then consider what a 'good enough' teacher would be like.

One group of induction tutors I worked with decided that a good enough NQT would have many of the characteristics in Figure 2.6. They did not expect any one person to have all of them but felt that a 'not good enough teacher' would be noticeably lacking in a fair number. Interestingly, many of the characteristics were not mentioned in the standards. For instance, the induction tutors thought that liking children was of prime importance and yet it does not feature in any standards, possibly because it is hard to measure and maybe it is assumed to be a given. Yet, we have met some teachers who do not particularly enjoy being with children of a certain age group.

Characteristics of a 'good enough' newly qualified teacher

Likes and is interested (rather than irritated by or scared of) the age group they teach
Enthusiasm
Flexibility
Open
Can admit mistakes
Wants to teach
Works hard
Respects the children, parents, support and teaching staff
Reflective
Can evaluate teaching and learning
Listens well
Approachable
Has high but realistic expectations
Stamina and good health
Punctual
Good attendance
Well organised – especially in planning and preparation
Knowledge of the curriculum
Can manage children
Sense of humour
Work in a team but shows initiative
Able to accept praise and positive criticism
Confident
Behaves professionally
Performs legal duties
Displays children's work

Figure 2.6 Characteristics of 'good enough' newly qualified teacher

Deciding which criteria to use

Having looked at a range of criteria for judging teachers it is important to come to a shared school view of what is most useful in your context. You might choose to use just one set of criteria or a combination of several. Clearly everyone whose teaching is to be monitored needs a clear understanding of the criteria on which they are being judged.

In a way the criteria are easy, because they describe teaching. What is harder and yet essential is to think about *how* these features are achieved and performance thus improved (Montgomery 1999, p.9). Equally it is useful to have some sort of breakdown of each criteria into levels, such as those we use in judging children's attainment in relation to the National Curriculum. This is one of the interesting features of the Hay McBer research because they do just that with the professional characteristics.

Activity 2.2
The 'good enough' teacher

In discussion with colleagues, make a list of the characteristics of what you would consider to be a good enough teacher. Think about what a 'not good enough teacher' would be like, so that you get a feel for the borderline area.

What differences are there between a good enough teacher and good enough newly qualified teacher?

How much match is there between your characteristics and published criteria?

Were you and your colleagues in agreement about the characteristics of a good enough teacher? What are the implications of areas of dispute?

Activity 2.3

Which criteria will your school use for judging the quality of teaching?

How can you link them with children's progress?

Are the criteria identified in the performance management policy?

How will you go about ensuring that all teaching staff have a clear understanding of what the criteria mean in practice?

Levels of professional characteristics

Hay McBer describe different levels for each of the professional characteristics. These can be very useful in moving people on in a structured way. For example, under Challenge and Support the scale develops in terms of the degree of firmness demonstrated in the support teachers give pupils, and the challenges they need to issue in the best interests of their pupils. At the lowest level this characteristic is about caring for pupils in a practical, immediate way. The second level combines challenge and support through the teacher expressing positive expectations of pupils. The higher levels express care for the pupils through the teacher's striving to secure the best possible provision for them, and challenging others to do likewise.

Levels for Challenge and Support (Hay McBer 2000)
1. Cares for the pupil
Ensures the day-to-day practical well-being and safety of pupils. Does not tolerate bullying and tackles it immediately.

2. Expresses positive expectations
Says to pupils 'You can do it'. Builds self-esteem in pupils by, for example, setting tasks which will allow them to succeed, giving rewards which are valued, and praising them when they have done well.

3. Strives for the best possible provision
Acts relentlessly in the interests of all pupils. Strives to secure the best possible provision. Persists in working for the best possible educational outcomes for all pupils, even when the going gets tough.

4. Challenges others in the pupil's best interests
Challenges others to bring about the best educational outcome for *all* pupils, persisting in overcoming barriers. Is prepared to be appropriately stern in the best interests of the pupil.

Levels for Managing Pupils (Hay McBer 2000)
1. Gets pupils on task
Quickly gets pupils on task, beginning lessons by stating learning objectives. Recaps and summarises points covered. Provides clear instructions about tasks and focuses pupils' attention.

2. Keeps pupils informed
Makes sure pupils understand why they are doing something. Describes how the activity fits into a programme of work. Keeps pupils up-to-date by providing information and feedback on progress.

3. Makes every class effective
Consistently makes any class or group effective by getting the right pupils working together on appropriate things. Removes barriers which are preventing the class or groups working effectively together.

4. Takes actions on behalf of the class
Speaks positively about the class to others and builds up its image. Goes out of his or her way to obtain the extra materials and resources the class, group or team needs: for example, by engaging the support of parents, the community or commercial organisations.

5. Takes the role of leader
Ensures the class and groups fully achieve their objectives at all times. Fully motivates *every* pupil and gets everyone wholly involved in achieving what needs doing. Always establishes a positive, upbeat atmosphere and takes pupils forward together.

The weakness of these level descriptions, however, is that they start at a pretty high level. For instance, the lowest level for managing behaviour expects that the teacher:

> Quickly gets pupils on task, beginning lessons by stating learning objectives. Recaps and summarises points covered. Provides clear instructions about tasks and focuses pupils' attention.

This is not very helpful for teachers who do not achieve this rather perfect description, but are at an earlier stage.

Awareness of the stages that teachers go through

In addition to thinking about what a good teacher is in your particular school setting, you should also consider what stage the teachers you are working with are at. There are recognised stages that new teachers go through. Recognising them will help you realise that teachers need different levels and types of support at different times. We have used Maynard and Furlong's (1993) five stages of development that beginning teachers go through to illustrate teachers' development (see Figure 2.7).

Stages that new teachers experience	
Stage	**Characteristics**
Early idealism	Feeling that everything is possible and having a strong picture of how you want to teach ('I'll never shout'). Bullough (1989) refers to this the 'fantasy' stage where teachers imagine pupils hanging on their every word.
Survival	Reality strikes. You live from day to day, needing quick fixes and tips. You find it hard to solve problems because there are so many of them. Behaviour management is of particular concern – you have nightmares about losing control. You are too stressed and busy to reflect. Colds and sore throats seem permanent. Survival often characterises this stage.
Recognising difficulties	You can see problems more clearly. You can identify difficulties and think of solutions because there is some space in your life. You move forward. This stage is aided considerably by a skilled team leader.

© Bubb and Hoare 2001

Figure 2.7 Five stages that new teachers experience (based on Maynard and Furlong 1993)

Hitting the plateau	Key problems, such as behaviour management and organisation, have been solved so you feel things are going well. You feel you are mastering teaching. You begin to enjoy it and don't find it too hard, but you don't want to tackle anything different or take on any radical new initiatives. If forced you will pay lip-service to new developments.
	Some teachers spend the rest of their career at this stage, but eventually their effectiveness deteriorates because they are not keeping up with new developments and changes in the curriculum. They may become failing teachers.
Moving on	You are ready for further challenges. You want to try out different styles of teaching, new age groups, take more responsibilities. If your present school does not offer sufficient challenge you will apply for a new job.

© Bubb and Hoare 2001

Figure 2.7 *cont.*

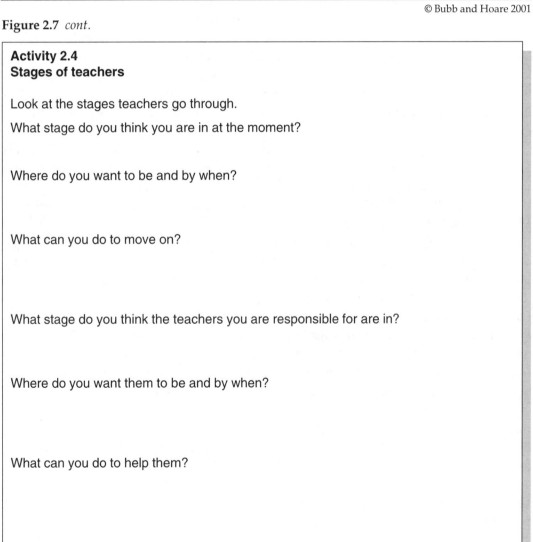

Activity 2.4
Stages of teachers

Look at the stages teachers go through.

What stage do you think you are in at the moment?

Where do you want to be and by when?

What can you do to move on?

What stage do you think the teachers you are responsible for are in?

Where do you want them to be and by when?

What can you do to help them?

Having considered criteria for judging teachers and the stages they are at, it is important to think about how to monitor. This is the subject of the next chapter.

3 How to monitor

Finding a focus

Monitoring the quality of teaching in isolation will in the long run achieve very little. Monitoring is a tool for improvement but there needs to be a clear vision about where the school is going, and there needs to be discussion about what school priorities will be achieved by a programme of teacher observation. A successful programme of school improvement depends on accurate monitoring within an overall approach. Monitoring therefore needs to target areas that have been identified as in need of improvement. Those monitoring could use a format such as the one in Figure 3.1 which enables people to write their own prompts having chosen a focus to look at. A useful starting point is the analysis of prior data: test results or work sampling for example.

The monitoring of teaching needs to be based on shared understandings of what is expected, so there is much preparatory work involved in staff discussion, debate and the formulation of school policy on the different aspects of teaching. Most schools use variations on the OFSTED criteria, the formats laid out in the model Performance Management Policy or the Hay McBer research commissioned by the DfEE. Details of these appear elsewhere in the book. However, it is insufficient to start with this type of checklist without ensuring that all staff fully understand what is expected by 'regular marking' for example. Management needs to supply information on what they expect from staff, what constitutes 'satisfactory teaching' in the context of the particular school.

There are a range of prerequisites that schools need to consider before they embark on monitoring. These systems and approaches are largely part of the approaches expected and implied by performance management and by Investors in People. The bottom line is 'good communication': employees have to know what the employer's expectation is before they stand a chance of fulfilling it. There needs to be wide-ranging discussion about this; opportunities for individuals to improve; resources provided by the employer to assist the employee. The first stage is for the organisation, in this case a school, to learn to know itself, analyse its strengths and weaknesses and prioritise targets for the short, medium and long term. It simultaneously needs to communicate this process to its employees. The following sections are an outline of how this might be achieved.

Monitoring Form		
Teacher: **Date:** **Monitor:** **Focus:**		
Prompts	**OK**	**Comments**
Overall judgement		

Figure 3.1 Pro forma for monitoring

Self-evaluation

Detailed guidance on self-evaluation is available from a range of sources. The DfEE website (www.dfee.gov.uk) contains a wide range of information that schools may use to analyse the data that is now available. The information in the 1999 PANDA (Performance Assessment National Data) Annexe is of particular interest in terms of the explanation of how SATs results may be converted to points scores. The 2000 PANDA assumes that the reader has a familiarity with the detail. As a document it is extremely useful as a tool for analysing one's school's results, but without the 1999 information it may be a little obscure.

The full process of school self-review and evaluation can be found at the back of the OFSTED Framework (1999a). You can start the process at a low level and build up towards it through a series of meetings that gradually lead staff forward. An important part of the process is the development of professional confidence in a particular curriculum area and this is best achieved through discussion, and through comparing systems, rather than forcing through a preferred system. The staff need to feel part of a group that is working together, supporting each other and which is committed to improvement. This feeling cannot be called into existence instantly. It needs to be developed over time.

This means that self-evaluation should be a regular curriculum management activity. All teachers and all coordinators should be involved in the process. It should be made up of ongoing checking and monitoring activities to ascertain the answer to the question: 'Are we doing what we said we'd do?' To put it simply : 'Is the school development plan for this area working?'

Such a programme should not be undertaken without an understanding of how important this is and how time-consuming. Performance management means the performance of all the members of the community or organisation. In the case of a school, this means not only the teachers but also the pupils, all the support staff and the governing body. At school level, it is likely to include a wholesale review of everything the school does and how it does it. This will begin with a consideration of what is taught through the programmes of study, how it is taught, what the school community understands by teaching and learning, and how information is transmitted between teacher and pupil. Performance management will permeate right down to the level of the marking policy for example, because oral and written feedback are the key communication between teacher and pupil.

Monitoring the curriculum through reviewing programmes of study

A way to monitor the curriculum is to review the programmes of study (see Figure 3.2).

Monitoring teaching and learning

Having begun with a review of the current schemes of work, it will be possible to consider how school review can be applied more generally. Applied as a whole, these questions would make up a detailed review agenda. Such a full-scale review might come about in a variety of ways:

Questions	Comments
Does the scheme of work indicate knowledge/ content to be covered over specific periods of time for the cohort/class so that coverage of the programme of study is ensured over the key stage?	
Does it set out the activities which pupils will be engaged in?	
Does it clearly define the learning objectives for the unit? Learning objectives should give some indication of the level of difficulty of the work, the range of attainment catered for and possibilities for differentiation.	
Are there clear references to the time needed for each unit of work?	
Does the scheme of work indicate aspects which will need to be assessed, particularly in subjects where work will not be revisited for some time?	
Does it define skills to be taught and developed over specific periods of time?	
Is there evidence of progression in the skills and content to be taught and learned?	
Is there evidence of a balanced range of skills to be taught?	
Does it ensure that a broad range of resources and media will be used?	
Does it indicate aspects of work which will be ongoing over the year, particularly in maths, English and ICT and which aspects will be taught in specific blocks of time during the year?	
Does it give staff some guidance on how to differentiate the work in the subject to ensure effective learning?	
Does it link effectively with work planned in other subjects and any cross-curricular themes, skills or dimensions?	

Figure 3.2 Monitoring the programmes of study

- as part of a planned review cycle linked to performance management and the school development plan;
- as a result of concerns about the effectiveness of the scheme in promoting high standards;
- as a response to changes in the statutory requirements for individual subjects;
- as a result of changing emphases in the curriculum as a whole or in individual subjects.

Using one of the various teaching observation forms available, staff may discuss what they understand by each specific heading. They need to understand how they show good subject knowledge and understanding in the way they present and discuss their subject. As a group it will help staff to debate what constitutes technical competence in teaching basic skills like phonics. The school as a whole also needs to consider what constitutes effective planning and how objectives can be shared with pupils appropriately. The more hidden aspects of teaching are the way teachers challenge and inspire their pupils; the way they communicate their high expectations to pupils in a way that encourages them to achieve through deepening their knowledge and understanding. The range of teaching methods used might also usefully be considered; different circumstances require different approaches, and shared staff discussion not only develops techniques, but also broadens understanding. Class management is another area that staff should discuss, so that all teachers and support staff are fully aware of the school behaviour policy, how to implement it and how to use it sensitively to manage pupils well. The use of time, support staff and resources, particularly computers, should be considered, safety issues shared and the aspects relating to equal opportunities fully debated. The school assessment policy must be clear and fully understood by all staff.

The other half of the process is learning, an area all too often neglected. Within lessons teachers should be encouraged to consider the extent to which pupils acquire new knowledge and new skills, develop ideas and increase their understanding. Teachers should also be encouraged to ask themselves why certain children apply intellectual, physical or creative effort in their work, and others seem not to do so, or to a lesser extent. Similarly, is it always a 'given' that a particular child works productively and at a good pace, or are there underlying reasons why they do not? Learning is the work of children: teachers should consider why it is that children show an interest in their work, are able to sustain concentration and show that they can think and learn for themselves. It is also most important that children understand what they are doing, how well they have done and how they can improve.

The culmination of this ongoing debate is the development of a shared understanding of what it means to be a teacher and a learner in a particular school. *En route*, a range of other aspects need to be covered, hammering out shared understandings among the teachers about how one actually arrives at different aspects of understanding teaching and learning.

Ways to monitor

The monitoring of teaching can be carried out in a wide range of ways and through a wide range of personnel. It is a mistake to consider that monitoring can only take place in a classroom during lesson time. This is important, but without proper preparation of the staff will achieve little. Constantly measuring someone does not make them grow: measurement is the check that proper nourishment and exercise has had its natural effect. Similarly with teaching: the provision of time for debate with colleagues, for the exchange of expertise and the development of professional understanding will have far greater and more beneficial effects on the quality of teaching than observation alone.

Team leaders need to monitor the teacher's progress. There are different ways to do this, as illustrated in Figure 3.3. Observation of teaching is a crucial form of evidence, but cannot be used to monitor everything. To illustrate this point, Figure 3.4 highlights some of the different forms of evidence for each of the induction standards that NQTs have to meet. Clearly in most primary schools team leaders can gain a good idea about the quality of a teacher through their everyday behaviour and work, but it is important that there is concrete evidence to discuss.

Working with adults

Team leaders are chosen because, among other things, they are good teachers. But good teachers of children may not necessarily be good teachers of adults. Many of the skills of teaching children, however, can be transferred to working with adults. Here are some similarities and differences that would be useful to consider.

What is different about teaching adults, rather than children?

The relationship between adults is more equal. On the surface, all adults will seem 'equal' but in practice all manner of power games may come into play. Usually inexperienced teachers will feel inferior. However, they may have more academic qualifications than other staff. A great many will have more up-to-date theoretical knowledge because they will have had to cover the demanding Initial Teacher Training National Curricula for English, mathematics, science and ICT. Some will be older than their team leader.

It can be very uncomfortable, humbling and potentially threatening when you are being the team leader for someone who is already a better teacher than you will ever be. It can also be extremely exciting, and cause one to improve one's own teaching. Many team leaders speak of how they benefit from helping teachers, not only because they reflect on their own practice but because they gain new insights and ideas.

Instead of a class of 30, the team leader normally only works with two or three teachers. This leads to more friendship and intimacy, which is usually a bonus, but can lead to the relationship becoming intense. Strong friendships develop, which might inhibit the team leader from pointing out areas for development in an objective way.

Clearly you cannot be bossy with adults. Tempting as it may seem, you cannot really tell them off, reward them with a sticker or punish them with a missed playtime. Sometimes you have to skirt around issues, hoping that dropping hints will be enough. Most adults behave well, understand what you are saying and respond well to advice. Some, however, have special needs and may require the same thing said in several different ways!

Form of monitoring	Advantages	Disadvantages
Observation	Detailed picture of what goes on in someone's classroom. Concrete evidence of the impact of teaching on learning. Reassures teachers that they are OK. Strengths celebrated and specifics can be discussed.	Stressful for teachers. Has to happen in the school day – cover issues. Time-consuming. Some people put on a show, others are too nervous to teach well. Can any lesson be typical?
Monitoring planning	Can happen outside the school day. Gives a good overview for continuity and progression. Can check that parallel classes are receiving the same curriculum. Can spot problems such as weak learning objectives and activities.	Advantages people who plan on paper in detail. Time-consuming.
Monitoring assessment	Can happen outside the school day. Clear picture of school and individual attainment and progress.	Advantages people who assess on paper in detail. Can be difficult to judge without knowledge of context.
Sampling children's work	Can happen outside the school day. Gives a good picture of what the children have done and the progress they have made – the results of the teaching. Gives insight into marking and teacher feedback. Useful to compare classes in same year group and to check against the planning.	Time-consuming. Need to know what you're looking for and stay focused. Hard to understand the work without knowing the context it took place in, how long children took to do it. Not so easy to do in the foundation stage.
Analysing test data	Can happen outside the school day. Clear picture of summative achievement. OFSTED inspections use the data to judge the school.	Statistics hide the real children. Not everything can be tested. Children's test everyday performance can differ.
Surveys	Can happen outside the school day. Can be used to discover views of staff, pupils and parents (360 degree feedback).	Do people answer honestly? Questions are hard to construct.
Display	Can happen outside the school day. Gives a picture of children's work that may not be in books such as in DT, art. Useful for monitoring ethos.	Hard to tell whether the work is representative of the ability range. Advantages teachers with skill in window dressing.
Informal exchanges with staff	Quick, immediate and often honest.	Depends on good open relationships.

Figure 3.3 Advantages and disadvantages to forms of monitoring

Induction Standard	Forms of evidence
(a) Sets clear targets for improvement of pupils' achievement, monitors pupils' progress towards those targets and uses appropriate teaching strategies in the light of this, including, where appropriate, in relation to literacy, numeracy and other school targets.	Planning Assessment file Observation Pupils' work
(b) Plans effectively to ensure that pupils have the opportunity to meet their potential, notwithstanding differences of race and gender, and taking account of the needs of pupils who are: • underachieving; • very able; • not yet fluent in English; making use of relevant information and specialist help where available.	Planning Observation Pupils' work Special needs assistants
(c) Secures a good standard of pupil behaviour in the classroom through establishing appropriate rules and high expectations of discipline which pupils respect, acting to pre-empt and deal with inappropriate behaviour in the context of the behaviour policy of the school.	Observation Display of class rules
(d) Plans effectively, where applicable, to meet the needs of pupils with special educational needs and in collaboration with the SENCO makes an appropriate contribution to the preparation, implementation, monitoring and review of Individual Education Plans.	Planning Assessment file Observation IEPs Pupils' work Discussion with SENCO and SNA
(e) Takes account of ethnic and cultural diversity to enrich the curriculum and raise achievement.	Planning Observation Looking at the classroom
(f) Recognises the level that a pupil is achieving and makes accurate assessments, independently, against attainment targets, where applicable, and performance levels associated with other tests or qualifications relevant to the subject(s) or phase(s) taught.	Assessment file Agreement trialling
(g) Liaises effectively with pupils' parents/carers through informative oral and written reports on pupils' progress and achievements, discussing appropriate targets, and encouraging them to support their children's learning, behaviour and progress.	Reports Letters to parents Notes from parents' evenings
(h) Where applicable, deploys support staff and other adults effectively in the classroom, involving them, where appropriate, in the planning and management of pupils' learning.	Planning Observation Discussion with support staff
(i) Takes responsibility for implementing school policies and practices, including those dealing with bullying and racial harassment.	Observation in lessons and around the school and playground
(j) Takes responsibility for their own professional development, setting objectives for improvements, and taking action to keep up-to-date with research and developments in pedagogy and in the subjects they teach.	Discussion Self-reflection Behaviour in meetings

© Bubb and Hoare 2001

Figure 3.4 Ways to monitor an NQT's progress against the induction standards

Adults have a great deal of 'baggage' compared with children. Most teachers have enormously high expectations of themselves and can quickly lose self-confidence when things do not go right. Some will have had damaging experiences at school that will call for sensitivity when commenting on a teacher's spelling mistakes, for instance.

Adults, like children, have home lives that may be less than ideal. Almost all teachers now join the profession in quite serious financial debt because of having to borrow money while at university. It is easy for established teachers to forget that, though not rich, they are more comfortably off than others. Many will be living in poor shared accommodation, have little money for transport, food, clothes and extras. Some have appallingly long and difficult journeys on public transport that significantly increase the length and stress of their working day. Inevitably teachers' personal relationships become strained, especially when they are too drained from a day's teaching to respond to loved ones and see friends.

Lessons to learn from working successfully with children

1. If we think about the way we like to be treated as adults and how children learn best, we will be better team leaders.
2. See your role as someone who allows the teacher to reflect off and who asks the questions that encourage them to think of the solutions themselves. A quotation that I find immensely powerful is:

> A leader is best
> When people barely know he exists,
> Not so good when people obey him and acclaim him,
> Worst when they despise him.
> But of a good leader, who talks little,
> When his work is done, his aim fulfilled,
> They will all say 'We did this ourselves'.
>
> Lao-Tse

3. Aim to be person-centred in the same way that as teachers we are child-centred. Think of their needs and interests. This, of course, must be married with the need to conform to the Performance Management policy and school philosophy, in the same way as children have to work within the National Curriculum.
4. Be sensitive to their beliefs and educational philosophy. There are many ways to teach children. You may not teach like they do, but that does not mean you are right – the proof is in the progress the children make.
5. Children and adults alike thrive on praise. Accentuate the positive and people will be more open to hearing the negative. Say something nice and the world turns more smoothly.
6. People think of their own solutions to problems if they are given structures such as focused time to think about the issue and someone to ask guiding open-ended questions and discuss with.
7. No one learns well when they are tired, hungry, ill, unhappy or stressed – keep an eye on the staff.
8. Make instructions and expectations clear. In a school people sometimes give different messages.

9. Like children, adults learn by being shown and having the opportunity to see others doing it right.
10. People thrive when they are treated with respect. They do not make progress when intimidated or when they feel a failure.

Activity 3.1
Remembering someone who helped you be a better teacher

Think of a colleague who made a difference to you; someone who inspired you, kept you going, etc.

List some of their characteristics or things they did that helped you become a better teacher.

In the next chapter we shall look in more depth at how to analyse data.

4 Analysing data on pupil performance

Statutory assessment

Many teachers do not fully realise their responsibilities in relation to how the school tackles statutory assessment and how it interprets these results. The expectations on teachers have steadily risen over the last few years, and at the very least teachers need to be familiar with the recent DfEE publications *Getting the Most from your Data* (DfEE 1999b) and *Recognising Progress – Getting the most from your data* (DfEE 2000c). Schools engage in a range of statutory procedures, starting with baseline assessment. The consultation document (DfEE 2000b) indicates that baseline assessment may be moved to the end of the Reception Year and that schools will need to develop an entry record from the beginning of a child's school career. Inspections and LEAs are routinely using baseline assessment as a predictor for Key Stage 1 SATs, and these are in turn used as predictors for Key Stage 2. The mandatory targets for children aged 11 feed through this process also: National Foundation for Educational Research (NFER) regularly produces indicators for future SATs performance based on baseline assessment. This is part of the 'Signposts' package (Birmingham LEA 2000). It is important that the teachers gain understanding about how and why these targets are set because their performance management targets are likely to be linked to them.

But equally, teachers need to put the process in perspective and must never become too hung up on figures. There are some situations where test results paint an inaccurate picture, such as with widely differing cohorts. Two autistic pupils in a year group of a junior school, for example, might distort the test results so that the whole year appears to be underachieving. This is an issue that has been recognised by many governing bodies and the solution could be to create a controlled sample taken from across the ability range to see how a similarly composed group performs over time.

Assessment systems

Schools use a wide range of assessment systems, some unique to the school, others available as proprietary systems. The first step is to discuss what systems are used in your particular school for assessment. When developing staff perception of an area as contentious as assessment in the context of performance management, it is vital to establish a firm grounding of 'Where we are now?' It is also important to reassure teachers, to remind them that they have achieved a great deal, and that they are building on what they already know. Schools are developing a wide range of different approaches to assessment, which come under two main headings: day-to-day assessment, and the statutory assessment required by the government. It is this perception that needs to be developed, so that teachers realise that they are using skills they already have but for a new purpose.

Teachers are accustomed to assessing learning at class level to target their planning and to meet the needs of individual children. This form of assessment looks forward to the next steps in children's learning and in many ways this is arguably the most important part of assessment so far as the business of teaching is concerned.

Many teachers are uncomfortable with the longer term use of assessment when it is used to set targets for the key stage, for the year group and for the individual class. There is a level of personal accountability implied here which is vital for pupils, but very threatening to teachers. At the back of the teacher's mind is always the thought, 'What if I don't meet the target?'

Teachers need to be able to contextualise their assessment practices and the achievements of the children in their class within the context of the school as a whole. There are many ways they can do this.

Figures 4.1 and 4.2 have a series of exercises to help teachers increase their knowledge of performance data.

Using the Internet to find out information about your school

Access the OFSTED website and look at the report for your own school and also for neighbouring schools, both schools in the same phase, and also schools from which you take pupils and to which you send them.
 Hyperlink http://www.OFSTED.gov.uk
 The reports are found under 'reports/index.htm'

The format of the reports will depend on when the school was last inspected and also on how well it is doing in relation to similar schools. The last report may have been the result of a short or of a full inspection. Look carefully at the parents' summary and the table that gives national and similar school comparisons. You will need to find out where the information about ethnicity, free school meals and special educational needs are located. Inspection reports all follow a similar outline, so once you have found one set of figures, you will be able to find this data more easily in other reports.

This information will help you form some ideas for the basis of your discussions. Some of the issues which might be discussed are:

- How did the school perform in particular subject areas (on the basis of prior attainment and using benchmark data)?
- How have pupils performed in relation to their prior attainment overall and for particular groups, e.g. boys and girls, ethnic minorities?
- How did our pupils perform in comparison with children from a similar school?
- Are some groups of pupils performing better than others? If so, why?
- How do the school's achievements compare with its previous achievements?
- Have some subject results shown marked improvement this year?
- Can any particular teaching and learning practices be identified to have contributed to successful results in certain areas?
- Are any of these features appropriate to use across the whole school and particularly in subjects where results are below the national average?

© Bubb and Hoare 2001

Figure 4.1 Using the Internet to find out information about your school

---

- Are there any trends that can be found in the PANDA which indicate action that needs to be taken by the head?
- What then are the emerging priorities for the school as a whole, and for the different coordinators?
- Do the figures for teacher assessment broadly match the test results?
- Find out what the actual pupil numbers were: does this affect the way you view the data when it is presented as percentages?

© Bubb and Hoare 2001

Figure 4.1 *cont.*

Finding out about school assessment policy and practice using school performance data

Talk to your colleagues in school about assessment policy and practice so that you understand about whole-school approaches and the implications for each class teacher and across different subjects.

- Find out about the use of tests, they may be formal or informal, throughout the school.
- Read the local data about the use of target setting in your LEA.
- Discuss aspects of school performance data with colleagues: the performance of boys in writing, the achievement of different ethnic groups.
- Put your school results in the local and national context, so that you develop your skill in interpreting data.
- Understand how test results are used for target-setting.
- Read inspection information and the school development plan.

© Bubb and Hoare 2001

Figure 4.2 Finding out about school assessment policy and practice using school performance data

Potential sources of school level data

The following list from the DfEE website (www.dfee.gov.uk) is a guide to the sources of information which may be useful. It is not exhaustive nor will every item be relevant to your school but it will give you an idea of what the likely sources might be.

Pupil progress

- OFSTED (Office for Standards in Education)
- LEA (Local Education Authority)
- EAZ (Education Action Zone)
- PIPS (Performance Indicators in Primary Schools)
- PANDA (Performance Assessment National Data)
- QUASE (Quantitative Analysis for Self Evaluation)
- Autumn Package (Pupil performance information on national basis)
- SATS (Key Stage Assessments)
- Pupil assessment (CATS – Cognitive Ability Tests)
- SDP (School Development Plan)

- Observation (Meetings, visits to school)
- Documentation, e.g. report to governing body/policy papers/letters
- Expert and professional advice (the adviser/inspectors/consultants/assessor)
- Survey
- Specific reports, e.g. IiP assessment/commissioned reports

Once staff are familiar with the big picture given by a general understanding of OFSTED reports, it may be helpful to review the potential sources of data available at school level. Schools have become increasingly expert in recent years in looking at the progress of their pupils' academic progress over time. The Autumn Package is sent to all schools and is available at www.dfee.gov.uk/statistics/DB/AUT under the heading 'performance'. It enables schools to compare themselves with schools of similar background and to study the extent to which they are performing above or below the levels expected by virtue of the background of their pupils. Results are moving more and more towards expression as 'points scores'. (See Figure 4.3 for point score guidance.) The Autumn Package contains the Key Stage 2 results expected from pupils of different average points scores in the Key Stage 1 tests taken four years earlier. It is likely that in the future this system may be extended to include data from baseline assessment taken from the point of entry to statutory schooling at age five.

OFSTED

OFSTED attempts to quantify the 'value added' to pupils by teachers by examining how well the school performs when compared with others of a similar background. Schools are placed in benchmark groups based on the percentage of full-time pupils known to be eligible for free school meals (FSM). The benchmark groups are as follows:

0–8%
9–20%
21–35%
36–50%
50%+

Thus if your school has 18 per cent of pupils eligible for FSM you will be compared with schools who have between 9 and 20 per cent FSM. At the present time, 'similar background' is limited to free school meals, but on this basis only a very partial picture of pupils' achievement can be developed. Yet this does not detract from the importance of OFSTED's findings: recent research (2000d) indicates that the education system is failing Afro-Caribbean students most appallingly. It is the statistics which can help us to find out where and why this happens and then do 'something about it'.

> That any ethnic group could enter school 20 percentage points in advance of the average, but leave 21 points behind, opens up an important area for educational debate on ethnic minority attainment. (OFSTED 2000d)

Average point score guidance

Average point score guidance reproduced from the 1999 Autumn Package, sent to all schools and contractors.

As mentioned earlier in the annex, point scores replace average levels rthis year. This means we can no longer simply use last year's method of assigning a value of '1' for Level 1 and '2' for Level 2, etc.

Assigning Point Scores to Levels
The performance of an individual pupil can be represented in terms of progress along a scale.

A level is achieved when performance exceeds the minimum threshold mark for that particular subject/level combination. Therefore a pupil at say Level 3 performance is somewhere between the minimum threshold for Level 3 and the minimum threshold for Level 4.

To assist in the process of determining averages we have assigned some values to the level thresholds.

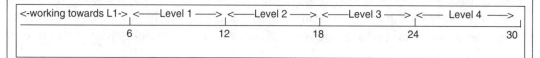

Since pupils will be distributed across the level we can similarly assign a points score equivalent to the mid-point of the relevant range.

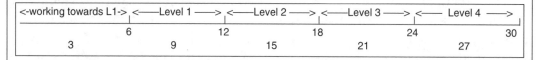

Hence a Level 1 would equate to 9 points, and a Level 3 to 21 points.

This concept can be extended to the differentiated breakdown of Level 2

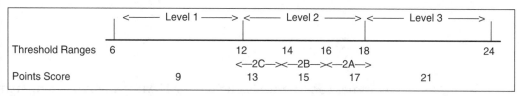

(Note that in the cases where the differentiated level within Level 2 was not calculated, or is not known, it would be appropriate to assign the value for the mid-point of the whole range, i.e. 15.)

To calculate an average across pupils to get a school average for benchmark purposes, you simply add together the relevant point scores and divide by the number of pupils.

Some Examples:
The average of a Level 1 and a Level 3 would be (9 + 21)/2 = 15
The average of a Level 2C and a Level 2A would be (13 + 17)/2 = 15
The average of two Level 2Cs and two Level 3s would be (13 + 13 + 21 + 21)/4 = 17
The average of two Level 4s and a Level 3 would be (27 + 27 + 21)/3 = 25

This method also allows one to compare the resultant points score average to Key Stage levels, although care must be taken with the interpretation: in the first two examples above the average points score is within the Level 2B range, and in the third example the average score is within the Level 2A range. In the fourth example, it is within the Level 4 range.

Figure 4.3 Average point score guidance 1999 Autumn Package

PANDA reports

OFSTED produces PANDA (Performance **AND A**ssessment) reports. These contain detailed information on the performance of pupils in the key stage assessments for the particular phase or phases of primary education for a particular school. They also contain analyses of whole-school performance and more detailed analysis of, for example, how boys and girls compare in their achievements over time and how individual subject areas compare with what could be expected from national samples of schools. This is an area where it is possible to have useful discussions with teachers: providing a curriculum that addresses gender differences positively is certainly something that they are expected to do and may well be one of the school targets to which they will be expected to contribute.

Statistical performance data

There are many possible sources of statistical performance data and these will vary from school to school. If your school does engage in some type of formal testing, it would be most useful to share this process fully with all teachers.

Some schools belong to groups which cooperate to produce robust data via a performance indicator system. The analysis of examination performance done through school membership of performance indicator systems operated by universities and research foundations such as PIPS (Performance Indicators in Primary Schools), MIDYIS (Middle Years Information System), and QUASE (Quantitative Analysis for Self Evaluation) can be of great value to a school. All these systems compare a school's 'actual' examination or test results with what would have been expected from pupils' prior levels of achievement. The size of the database and the rigorousness of the enquiry systems means that even the data for very young children has a test/retest validity of 0.9 (Tymms 1999). In other words, it is an extremely accurate indicator.

LEA comparisons

Many local education authorities analyse school performance for the schools in their areas. These provide valuable data as they examine the local picture in great detail, in a way that PANDA, for example, cannot. The format used usually shows how schools' actual levels of achievement are above or below what could be expected from their intakes of pupils, given the overall performance of all the pupils/schools in each LEA. These analyses are often detailed, even in the primary phase. The question mark lies against the use of baseline assessment for the purposes of 'value-added' by LEAs (and also during OFSTED inspections). There are currently 91 accredited baseline assessment systems. They are generally designed for observational assessment to be used to plan learning. They do not have a test/retest validity and therefore cannot be used to produce statistically valid 'value-added' information (Tymms 1999, Goldstein *et al.* 2000).

Blanket testing

Increasingly, schools are analysing performance and individual pupil achievement through school participation in 'blanket testing' of entire age cohorts of pupils. This may be accomplished in collaboration with other groups of schools in an LEA. Many LEAs carry out Year 7 tests to identify reading problems that require intervention by the school. Many junior schools administer similar tests, often of reading or literacy at the beginning of Year 3. In many ways these tests smack of mistrust between phases, and seem to be underpinned by the assumption that previous teachers have not done their job properly. Virtually all of these schemes involve feedback to schools of individual pupil results and overall school averages, usually by comparison with the performance of all the children/schools blanket tested in the LEA.

Commercially available systems

Many schools have routinely used commercially produced tests from a commercial test provider such as NFER (e.g. Cognitive Ability Tests (CATs)) to track pupil performance. These tests will usually have 'norms' as to the expected performance of pupils of various ages but do not as a rule have evidence about the levels of achievement to be expected from pupils of different backgrounds.

Example of analysis using NFER results
NFER 2000 quartile marks for each year group

	95th percentile	Upper quartile	Median	Lower quartile
Year 3 English Maths	131–123 135–127	122–117 125–121	115–100 120–103	99–78 101–81
Year 4 English Maths	142–123 140–124	122–118 121–118	115–99 117–103	96–75 102–73
Year 5 English Maths	131–120 136–124	117–113 123–116	112–92 115–99	90–71 98–70
Year 6 English Maths	138–126 139–130	124–117 129–120	116–98 119–102	97–73 101–79

The school has made up a table based on the current NFER results so that the senior management team can easily see the difference between year groups and the range of results across Key Stage 2. The table indicates that in these tests pupils were achieving at higher levels in maths than in English. Thus, an area for development would clearly be investigating the reasons behind the lower English results: gender differences? boys' writing? higher than average EAL? social factors? Clearly the next step is some detailed action research by the English coordinator to analyse the reasons.

Very often an investigation of what is being achieved by the middle ability band is very revealing. In the table of results above, the range of scores across the median band is good for maths in all year groups: is this the result of good planning and assessment? Do the teachers have particular strengths in this area? Is there a cohort factor in operation? The median for English is good in Year 3 and in Year 4, but is worryingly low in Year 5. The reasons for this should be explored by work sampling and by the direct monitoring of teaching as a matter of urgency. The Year 6 results are quite low also, and need investigation.

It is of course important to understand the reasons for the range of marks, as shown by the upper and lower quartile marks. However, this aspect is unlikely to alter relative to the rest of the school as the particular cohort progresses through a given key stage. Over time, one might well see a slight improvement in so far as the lower quartile is moved up relative to the other bands. The upper quartile, with challenging teaching and high expectations may well move ahead at a faster rate, thus broadening the spread of marks. When examining historic data from some schools, it is clear that over time the typical 'bell jar' curve of distribution has been shifted up the scale. The nature of special educational needs within a school may however mean that over time there is an increasingly long 'tail' of underachievement in relation to age-related norms.

In terms of performance management, the task of the head teacher is to ensure that the school is producing detailed analysis of test results in an accessible form, and to create the ethos which allows free debate on where standards need to be raised, but without blame or recrimination. The role of the senior management team is to assist the head teacher in collecting the information and informing it via classroom observation. Where they are also subject coordinators, there is a need to engage in detailed analysis of *why* things are as they are, and what can be altered to improve standards. The targets would feed down to class level through the classroom observation outcome discussion, through training and through school policies: for example, adherence to the behaviour management policy, following the marking policy, using the teaching and learning policy effectively.

The above analysis can be carried out using any assessment systems with retest validity. It is also possible to track the results of the voluntary tests at Years 3, 4 and 5.

Individual systems

Rather than wait for national systems, some schools have designed their own approach to the analysis of pupil performance. Such school-designed systems for pupil achievement data may be based on the linking of school or teacher assessment data to National Curriculum levels.

QCA tests

More than 90 per cent of all primary schools now utilise the optional tests that have been produced by QCA which can be administered at the end of Years 3, 4 and 5. All primary schools have been given detailed analysis of the progress of national samples of pupils over the four years of Key Stage 2, based upon an analysis of national samples of children. Government agencies and NGOs state that in the area of writing, for example, it is possible to look at the progress expected of children during each of Years 3, 4, 5, and 6 by looking at their start of year levels and at end of year levels. These agencies also contend that for reading and mathematics it is possible to calculate what reading or mathematics score is to be expected at the end of the year for each child utilising the child's finishing score from the previous year.

In the world of statistics, it is thus possible to predict the theoretical gain that a child might make in each term at school, and measure how far in advance or how far behind the expected rate of progress that particular pupil is. In the real world, where divorce, homelessness and all the other myriad horrors that beset children come into play, such notional progress may be laughable. The real story is of course, infinitely complex. It is part of the job of the school management to develop awareness among teachers that there are demanding, measurable expectations expressed through performance management, but at the same time emphasise the human side also. Teachers need to be fully aware of the demands and expectations coming from government and the local education authority and also to understand the shortcomings of the data. They need to be aware that the notional progress expected must be viewed in relation to the personal, social and emotional context of the individual child. In other words a holistic view is needed. Plus a healthy degree of realism.

Statutory requirements for assessment

You need to reflect with your teachers on how your school tackles the statutory requirements for assessment and how your school uses and interprets these results. It is also important that the teachers gain some understanding about how the school is setting targets in cooperation with the local education authority. In many schools, this will mean a detailed programme of familiarisation with the processes used across the school and in different key stages.

Key Stage 1 data

The younger the children the sparser the data. Many primary and infant schools collect additional data that can help evaluate pupils' progress. Some have their own systems of data collection and analysis. Many local authorities have additional testing schemes for reading and mathematics at Key Stage 1 in addition to the baseline arrangements. Some schools may be in performance indicator systems that permit the comparison of 'actual' achievement levels attained with those predicted by a school based upon prior achievement levels and/or its pupil backgrounds. But the main source of comparative data is the end of key stage SATs. The massive changes in the context and content of the tests is an irritation to teachers, but this misses the point. Where schools have tracked cohorts of children through their career at a particular school, the changes in the tests have been incidental. Teacher assessment in preceding years has informed and contextualised the test results and allowed schools to target particular groups and also individuals.

During recent years, baseline testing data has been used to give an indication of children's level of achievement when they arrive at the beginning of the key stage, with gain then to be assessed across the key stage. As Key Stage 1 teachers are well aware, the baseline assessments differ according to local education authority and some are more useful in terms of analysis than others.

The government contends that Key Stage 1 assessment data from The Autumn Package and the PANDA provides an end-point for the stage from which schools can be compared with the performance of all schools taking pupils from similar backgrounds. A very partial picture, some would say, but nevertheless, teachers need to be aware of the constraints and demands that government expectations put on them.

Children with special educational needs

Many children with special needs will be able to be, and have been, assessed on exactly the same range of assessment data as other children and have participated in the same key stage arrangements. They will therefore have start-point data and end of year data on which they can be assessed. If schools have additional data from performance indicator systems, their own testing or blanket testing schemes then children with special needs will show gain on them compared with their own baseline.

In most cases the national data systems are not sensitive enough to pick up the changes in achievement shown by such children. Individual Education Plans (IEPs) will provide a valuable source of information. In addition, in such cases the achievement expected may be more in their personal and social development than in their academic career. For such children, the criteria reported in *Supporting the Target Setting Process: Guidance for effective target setting for pupils with special educational needs* (DfEE 1998a) in the domains of language, literacy, mathematics and personal/social development are likely to be valuable. These involve the allocation of 'p' levels to children in the same way as they are allocated National Curriculum levels. Many schools are using the 'p' scales to good effect, finding that they can track progress accurately (DfEE 1998a).

Nursery

Most schools are likely to possess only internal school data on their pupils at this stage (although of course the baseline assessments recently begun with children provide a form of outcome of the nursery years). While some schools may use standardised testing of developmental stages and/or foundation level academic and social skills, for the great majority of schools the progress of children will be judged in terms of the school/teacher's assessments routinely conducted, on the early learning goals.

Target setting

Links between target setting and performance management

The statutory requirement to set targets for pupils' performance in English and mathematics at age 11 and 16 came into force in September 1998. This is part of the government's strategy for raising standards in schools. The corollary for staff is the requirement for performance management. The process for both these processes involves the monitoring of teaching and learning in some detail, albeit with a slightly different focus in terms of evidence gathering. As with so many new initiatives, the success of a school hinges upon the adaptability of the staff and the ability of senior management to see connections. With imagination and good planning, members of the senior management team can set the milestones for the school year, organise the programme of monitoring and devise an approach that allows them to collect robust and accurate data that may be used for a variety of purposes.

Targets for teaching

Performance management requires the setting of targets in the area of teaching, to define the ways that each teacher will achieve his or her share of the overall aims for learning of the school for that particular year or term. To monitor and evaluate the success of performance management, the process of target setting for the pupil, the group, the cohort, and the school needs to be evaluated and judgements made about relative success. It is important to continually test and retest hypotheses about what may or may not be achieved and to explore the reasons why some initiatives are more successful than others. The target setting process in the area of learning, will define the extent to which the teaching makes a difference to the achievement of each particular pupil.

The reason for target setting

The process of target setting is well established in schools. Good schools have been setting SMART (Specific, Measurable, Achievable, Realistic, Timed) targets for many years. This is one of the key features of good schools. The passing of legislation to make target setting a statutory requirement is evidence of an attempt by the government to spread this good practice to all schools.

Strategies for monitoring

Similarly the monitoring of teaching has been an established feature of the lives of many schools. Without it how can a head teacher, a year group leader or a subject coordinator know what is going on in his or her area? Schools can be creative places, the range of styles of monitoring varies enormously from setting to setting. The main styles are covered in this book. Broadly speaking, they can be divided into two main areas: *the monitoring of teaching* and *the monitoring of standards of work*.

Within these two broad areas, there are a number of subdivisions: the monitoring of the different levels of planning and the setting of targets for individuals, groups, classes, year groups, key stages and the school as a whole. The monitoring of standards of work may be split up into lesson observation of various types and scrutiny of work in a range of contexts.

The school improvement cycle

Schools are very familiar with the data and diagrams related to performance management. Many schools began to use systematic planning for improvement in 1999 when the *Getting the Most from your Data* document (DfEE 1999b) was first published. The familiar five-stage circle (see Figure 4.4) that is seen so frequently first appeared in that publication.

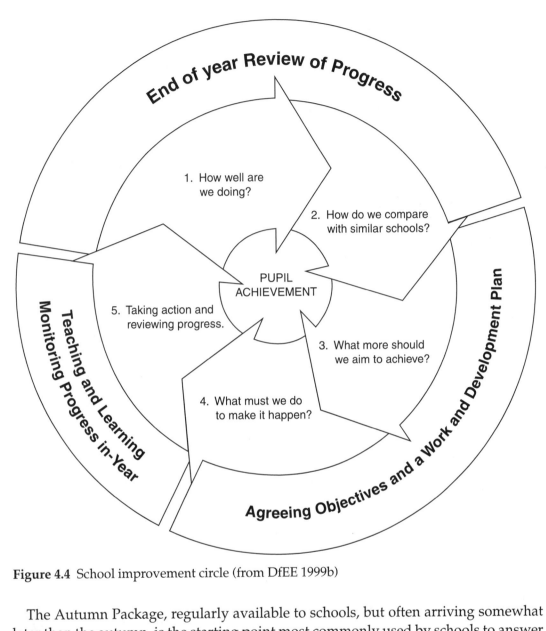

Figure 4.4 School improvement circle (from DfEE 1999b)

The Autumn Package, regularly available to schools, but often arriving somewhat later than the autumn, is the starting point most commonly used by schools to answer the first question on the circle, 'How well are we doing?' Teachers always have a very good idea of the current and ever-changing answer to this question so far as their own class is concerned. The trick is to develop and synthesise this class-level information in such a way that it illuminates the raw data in the Autumn Package. The method used to do this is to select the range of monitoring strategies that most effectively illustrate the achievements and the areas for the future development of the school.

The first areas to investigate are the content of the teaching. In the past, repetition of topic areas, especially between key stages was common, resulting for instance in pupils learning about the Romans three times, and at more or less the same level each time. Lack of liaison between year teachers and choices available under the old National Curriculum where teachers could select a topic they were interested in were to blame.

The main danger of this repetition is, however, the gaps. How often as a teacher have you embarked on a new area of mathematics for instance, only to realise with increasing horror that the lesson on data handling you have prepared assumed a prior knowledge and understanding in the pupils that they simply did not have? There are a range of reasons for this: the teacher may be labouring under a false set of expectations for this year group; perhaps this cohort has a significant special educational needs component which has slowed their progress; perhaps the pace of previous lessons was too swift, with insufficient time for consolidation. The hypothetical reasons are legion. Their range also indicates that monitoring the expected curriculum, the one planned in advance, may be insufficient. It may be necessary to examine the delivered curriculum, in the form of the teacher's short-term plans, and also check back on issues like absence and withdrawal. Is a particular group regularly missing part of the input because of attendance at other lessons targeted specifically at them? And, of course, pupils do not always absorb lessons in the way intended.

In the next chapter we shall look in detail at classroom observation as a key tool in monitoring teaching.

5 Classroom observation

Observation

Observation is a powerful tool for assessing and monitoring a teacher's progress. Used well, it can also be a way to support teachers, because observation gives such a detailed picture and enables very specific targets to be set. The value of observation, however, depends on how well it is planned, executed and discussed afterwards (Hagger and McIntyre 1994, p.10). It is almost always a stressful experience, not only for the teacher but also for the observer. The fewer observations a teacher has the greater the pressure for them to go well. They also need to be conducted fairly so that teachers like Paul and Jane are treated equally.

Case Studies
Paul's experiences

Paul was given a week's notice that his team leader, Lucy, was going to observe him. They planned the observation in detail and agreed that Lucy would focus on Paul's sharing of the learning objectives and how the pupils knew whether they had met them.

Paul found the run up to the observation stressful, but managed to prepare thoroughly. He had seen Lucy teach, and realised that she was very experienced. He felt very self-conscious at the start of the observation, and made a few mistakes as a result but relaxed when the team leader gave him a sympathetic smile. Overall, Paul thought the lesson went well and was relieved by Lucy's words of praise as she left the room.

They discussed the lesson at the end of that day. Paul was pleased that his achievements had been recognised. Lucy pointed out some strengths that he had not been aware of, which was gratifying. He agreed with what she identified as areas to develop and found it helpful to set objectives and action points to address them. He felt in safe hands.

Jane's experiences

Jane's head teacher gave her no warning that he was going to observe and they had not discussed what the focus should be. He arrived half way through the whole-class introduction and interrupted her to ask for a lesson plan. This threw her and she rushed her explanation of the activity which meant that the children were unsure what to do and misbehaved. The lesson went badly. The head teacher left without saying anything.

Ten days later Jane received some written notes about the lesson, but was unable to discuss it because the head teacher was too busy and she didn't want to make a fuss. She felt that some of the points were useful but was upset at the negative tone and long list of action points. She thought that judgements were being based on a lesson that was completely untypical. Jane felt that the observation had not only been a waste of time but gave a very damaging and unfair picture of her teaching, that she would have to work hard to rectify. Her stress levels increased.

Team leaders may also find observing stressful, because they feel inexperienced and uncertain of the best way to go about it. The year group and area of the curriculum to be taught may not be familiar. They may feel that the quality of their observation and feedback will compare unfavourably to that of others. As the person responsible for the teacher they will also be mindful of the need to move them forward while maintaining a good relationship. This can lead team leaders to be too kind, and to not bite the bullet. Teachers sometimes feel that they are not being sufficiently challenged, and the observation and feedback is only superficial. This is particularly true of the most successful teachers, but they too need to be helped to develop professionally.

Activity 5.1
Remembering what it is like to be observed

Think back to the times you have been observed.
What happened before the observation and how did you feel?

What happened during the observation and how did you feel?

What happened after the observation and how did you feel?

Bearing these experiences in mind, how do you want to go about making the observation and feedback?

Observation and giving feedback are very complex skills, skills which need training and practice. The important thing to remember is that the whole process needs to be useful for the teacher. It is for their benefit that it is being done. To this end it is essential that team leaders consider the context of the observation. This includes:

– the stage of the teacher;
– how they are feeling;
– their previous experiences of being observed;
– the state of the team leader's relationship with the teacher;
– what part of the school year, week and day it happens in; and
– the disposition of the class.

Team leaders also need to recognise their own values, beliefs and moods. When we were less experienced we had strong views on what we considered good teaching to be. With hindsight, this was very subjective, narrow and arrogant. This is why it is important to concentrate on the progress the children make before judging the effectiveness of the teaching. The more one observes other teachers, the more convinced one is that there is no one way to teach.

Observers should also recognise their own feelings at the time of the observation. No one functions effectively when they are tired, stressed or irritable. People tend to be more generous and easygoing when feeling happy. Team leaders must recognise their feelings, and in some way compensate for them, in order to be as objective as possible. They also need to recognise that their very presence in the classroom will affect the children. This is accentuated as the children will know them as another member of staff, perhaps even their former teacher.

Making an observation – things to consider

Choosing a focus

As with all monitoring it is useful if not essential to have a focus – something that you are looking at in particular. This will not exclude you from noticing and commenting on other things but will ensure that you have information on the key area that you are working on. This will depend on what your overall focus for monitoring is. In all cases, it should be linked to raising standards – helping children learn more effectively. Here are what some teachers chose as a focus.

Feedback to children (oral and written)
- How well do different groups know what they are doing?
- How well do different groups know why they are doing it?
- How do different groups know how well they have done?
- What sort of feedback does the teacher use, and to which children?

(For an exploration of Gipps *et al.* feedback taxonomy (1996) in reception classes, see Bubb and Burrell 2000.)

Learning objectives
- How well are these conveyed?
- Are they appropriate for different groups of children?
- Do the activities enable them to achieve the objectives?
- Do all children meet them well enough?

Management
- Does the teacher have good control at different parts of the lesson and of all the children?
- How do they manage off-task behaviour?
- Is there a brisk pace that keeps children's attention?
- Are resources appropriate, organised and distributed to make best use of time?

Before the observation

1. Agree a date and time in advance – a week's notice is reasonable. Choose a lesson that the teacher feels happy with and that will give you the information you need.
2. Agree how long you will be observing – a whole session is ideal, but this may not be necessary, depending on what you want to look at.
3. Ensure that both of you are clear about the purpose of the observation. Let teachers have a copy of the pro forma you will be using and the criteria you will be judging them by.
4. Discuss with the teacher what should be the focus of the observation. Relate the focus to progress in meeting their objectives and helping children learn more effectively.
5. Discuss ground rules such as how your presence is to be explained to the class, what you are going to do, where you should sit, your exact time of arrival.
6. Discuss what you will need before or at the beginning of the observation, such as the lesson plan and access to the planning file. If you need something in advance, agree when the teacher is going to give it to you.
7. Agree a time and place to discuss the lesson, giving yourself time to reflect and write notes, ideally within 24 hours of the observation.
8. Give the teacher a written copy of the arrangements, to avoid confusion.
9. To build up trust, arrange for the teacher to observe you teach before you watch them.
10. Be positive and optimistic, to aid the teacher's confidence.
11. Prepare the teacher for feedback by giving them tips such as suggested below.

Post-observation discussion – tips for the teacher
- You will almost always be asked how you thought the lesson went, so reflect on the lesson. In particular, think about the progress pupils made. What were you pleased with? What could have gone better? How typical was it? Do not be disheartened if the lesson didn't go well. See it as a one off event to be learnt from.
- Listen well. Don't just hear what you want or expect to hear. Focus on what is being said rather than how it is being said. See it as information rather than criticism and make notes of salient points.
- Explain reasons for doing something that might not have been clear to the observer – stick up for yourself.
- Try to summarise the observer's views, asking them if they agree. Ask for advice and ideas, and clarification of anything you are unsure of.
- Afterwards, reflect on the discussion. Feel good about the positive comments and think how to improve.

Choosing an observation format

There is no such thing as an ideal lesson observation pro forma, yet sometimes anything seems better than a blank piece of paper. Different formats will be useful at different times and for different situations. I have summarised the advantages and disadvantages of the most frequently used formats for lesson observation in Figure 5.1.

Observation format	Advantages	Disadvantages
1. OFSTED evidence form (OFSTED 1999a).	Good emphasis on the relationship between the teaching and the children's response and learning. The seven point grading might be useful in helping you decide whether the teaching and learning was good enough.	These may seem too formal and their association not conducive to how the team leader wants to be perceived. Hard to use if not familiar with the OFSTED criteria.
2. Participant observation – help the children while observing.	Reduces the stress on the teacher. Should benefit the children in that lesson.	Hard to participate and observe. You affect the dynamics through participating, and are not simply judging the teacher's work but your own too. It can also undermine the teacher's authority.
3. Observing without making notes.	Being released from the need to write enables the observer to see a great deal. Reduces the stress on the teacher.	Without the structure of some note making the observer can end up seeing everything and nothing. Can be idiosyncratic and not grounded in evidence.
4. Diary description – a running log of what happens in the lesson.	Gives lots of detail, that the teacher may be unaware of. This should ensure objectivity.	Observer writes reams – much of it not particularly useful. A video can describe the lesson objectively.
5. Running record with judgements, tips and questions.	Judgements are in context, which gives a clear picture, with reasons, for the teacher. Allows flexibility in writing about the things of most import.	Involves lots of writing. Depends on the skill and experience of the observer to pick out useful bits and make suggestions.
6. Timed event sampling – noting what happens every five minutes (see Figure 5.7).	Might give a good description of what went on in a lesson. Useful for tracking an individual child.	Involves lots of writing and not useful for giving the big picture. Observer might miss something because it does not happen at the right time.
7. Lesson structure forms – key points relating to mental/oral warm-up, plenary, etc.	Useful for seeing the effectiveness of different parts of a lesson. Good for literacy and numeracy coordinators to use to get an overview of how and which parts of the lesson are working well.	May not give a big picture. Can give too much emphasis on the structure rather than what is being learned.
8. Form with sections under a few headings (see Figure 5.11).	Keeps you focused on commenting on key areas that you can decide on before the lesson.	The size of the boxes may constrain you at times, and at other times make you feel that you are writing something for the sake of it.
9. Checklist – statements that you grade, tick or cross (see Figures 5.2, 5.3 and 5.6).	Easy for the observer to complete. Gives a big picture.	Does not give a flavour of the particular lesson. No examples. Does not give judgements – just says what was present.

Figure 5.1 Formats for lesson observation – advantages and disadvantages

Observation format	Advantages	Disadvantages
10. Checklist with judgements to mark (see Figure 5.5.)	Easy for the observer to complete. Gives a big picture.	Does not give a flavour of the particular lesson. No examples or reasons for judgements.
11. A sheet with teaching prompts (see (Figure 5.9 and 5.10).	Enables you to write about what seems most useful, but the prompts focus you on areas you need to consider. The prompts can be adapted according to the agreed focus of the lesson.	Depends on the skill and experience of the observer to pick out useful bits and make suggestions.
12. A sheet with learning prompts (see Figures 5.8)	Clear focus on the children's learning and what the teacher does to help or hinder it. Gives a good picture of for which children the teaching is being most effective.	Can become engrossed in what the children do rather than the teaching. Hard to pick out different groups within the class (boys, girls, different attainment, SEN, EAL).
13. Strengths and areas for development sheet (see Figure 5.12).	Gives a clear picture of your judgements because it just focuses on strengths and areas for development.	Needs to be backed up with evidence and examples. Unless you are very experienced, this is best used as a summary sheet after one of the formats above has been used.
14. List of action points (see Figure 5.4).	Clear what to improve.	Depressing list of things to do without any recognition of strengths and successes.

© Bubb and Hoare 2001

Figure 5.1 *cont.*

It is essential to look at teaching in relation to learning. One must always be thinking about cause and effect. Why are the children behaving as they are? The cause is often related to teaching. Thus, the observer needs to look carefully at what both the teacher and the children are doing. Too often the teacher gets most of the attention, yet the product of their work is the children's learning – the proof of the pudding. For note-taking purposes decide whether the main focus is going to be on the pupils and their learning and behaviour with the teaching as the cause, or whether the focus is the teacher with the children's learning and behaviour as the result.

Activity 5.2

Use different observation formats, perhaps using the same video of some teaching. Consider the merits and drawbacks of each format.

Which is easiest for you to use?

Which is the most useful?

Classroom Observation Checklist

Tick where you think professional development is needed.

Lesson planning and preparation
The lesson was part of a planned programme.
There was a good structure to the lesson.
The aims of the lesson were clear. Resources for the lesson were prepared and available.
Individual pupils' learning needs were taken into account.

Understanding of the subject area
A good understanding of the subject content covered in the lesson was displayed.

Teaching methods
Instructions and explanations were clear and specific.
Pupils were involved, were listened to, and were responded to appropriately.
The ideas and experiences of pupils were drawn upon. The teaching methods adopted were suitable for all pupils in the class.

The assessment and evaluation of pupils within the class
Pupils were involved and their understanding evaluated through the use of appropriate questioning. Mistakes and misconceptions were recognised by the teacher and were responded to within the lesson.

The management of pupil behaviour
Action was taken promptly to address inappropriate pupil behaviour. The teacher was confident in the strategy that he or she adopted for encouraging and rewarding good behaviour.
Where behaviour was inappropriate, the teacher knew the next steps to take.

The teacher's objectives for pupils' learning
Pupils understood what work was expected of them during the lesson.
Pupil outcomes of the lesson were consistent with the objectives set at the beginning.
The pace was appropriate.

Classroom observation
The classroom was well organised.
Appropriate materials were available to pupils when needed.
Where teacher assistants were involved, appropriate use was made of their support.

Homework
Homework was set in accordance with the school's homework policy.
Appropriate feedback on homework was given.

Figure 5.2 The NUT classroom observation checklist (NUT 2000)

Once you know your focus for the observation you can think of prompts which you can write on Figure 5.10 (p. 63).

Teaching Strategy Checklist	
Observer: Date:	
Teacher: Year group: _____	
Observation started _____ ended _____	
Subject and learning objective:	
Stimulating intellectual curiosity, communicating enthusiasm for the subject being taught, fostering pupils' enthusiasm and maintaining pupils' motivation.	
Matching the approaches used to the subject matter and the pupils being taught.	
Structuring information well, including outlining content and aims, signalling transitions and summarising key points as the lesson progresses.	
Clear presentation of content around a set of key ideas, using appropriate subject-specific vocabulary and well-chosen illustrations and examples.	
Clear instruction and demonstration, and accurate well-paced explanation.	
Effective questioning which matches the pace and direction of the lesson and ensures that pupils take part.	
Careful attention to pupils' errors and misconceptions, and helping to remedy them.	
Listening carefully to pupils, analysing their responses and responding constructively in order to take pupils' learning forward.	
Selecting and making good use of textbooks, ICT and other learning resources which enable teaching objectives to be met.	

© Bubb and Hoare 2001

Figure 5.3 Teaching strategy checklist

Action Points Observation Sheet
Observer: **Observation started** _____ **ended** _____
Teacher: **Date:**   **Year group:**
Subject and learning objective:
Action points:

Figure 5.4 Action points observation sheet

Lesson Observation: Assessment					
Date:		**Teacher:**			
Lesson:		**Observer:**			

	Excellent	Good	Satisfactory	Development Needed	N/A
1. The teacher plans effectively and sets clear objectives that are understood	☐	☐	☐	☐	☐
2. The teacher shows good subject knowledge and understanding	☐	☐	☐	☐	☐
3. The teaching methods used enable all pupils to learn effectively	☐	☐	☐	☐	☐
4. Pupils are well managed and high standards of behaviour are insisted upon	☐	☐	☐	☐	☐
5. Pupils' work is assessed thoroughly	☐	☐	☐	☐	☐
6. Pupils achieve productive outcomes	☐	☐	☐	☐	☐
7. The teacher makes effective use of time and resources	☐	☐	☐	☐	☐
8. Homework is used effectively to reinforce and extend learning	☐	☐	☐	☐	☐

Conclusions and feedback:

Strengths:

Areas for development:

Teachers comment (optional):

Figure 5.5 Lesson observation: assessment (from DfEE 2000e *Performance Management Model Policy*)

Lesson Observation Guidance

1. The teacher plans effectively and sets clear objectives that are understood
(a) Objectives are communicated clearly at the start of the lesson
(b) Materials are ready
(c) There is a good structure to the lesson
(d) The lesson is reviewed at the end
(e) The learning needs of those with IEPs are incorporated with the teacher's planning

2. The teacher shows good subject knowledge and understanding
(a) Teacher has a thorough knowledge of the subject content covered in the lesson
(b) Subject material was appropriate for the lesson
(c) Knowledge is made relevant and interesting for pupils

3. The teaching methods used enable all pupils to learn effectively
(a) The lesson is linked to previous teaching or learning
(b) The ideas and experiences of pupils are drawn upon
(c) A variety of activities and questioning techniques is used
(d) Instructions and explanations are clear and specific
(e) The teacher involves all pupils, listens to them and responds appropriately
(f) High standards of effort, accuracy and presentation are encouraged
(g) Appropriate methods of differentiation are used

4. Pupils are well managed and high standards of behaviour are insisted upon
(a) Pupils are praised regularly for their good effort and achievement
(b) Prompt action is taken to address poor behaviour
(c) All pupils are treated fairly, with an equal emphasis on the work of boys and girls, and all ability groups

5. Pupils' work is assessed thoroughly
(a) Pupil understanding is assessed throughout the lesson by the use of the teacher's questions
(b) Mistakes and misconceptions are recognised by the teacher and used constructively to facilitate learning
(c) Pupils' written work is assessed regularly and accurately

6. Pupils achieve productive outcomes
(a) Pupils remain fully engaged throughout the lesson and make progress in the lesson
(b) Pupils understand what work is expected of them during the lesson
(c) The pupil outcomes of the lesson are consistent with the objectives set at the beginning
(d) The teacher and pupils work at a good pace

7. The teacher makes effective use of time and resources
(a) Time is well utilised and the learning is maintained for the full time available
(b) A good pace is maintained throughout the lesson
(c) Good use is made of any support available, e.g. learning assistants and older pupils
(d) Appropriate learning resources are used, e.g. ICT

8. Homework is used effectively to reinforce and extend learning
(a) Homework is set if appropriate
(b) The learning objectives are explicit and relate to the work in progress
(c) Homework is followed up if it has been set previously

Figure 5.6 Lesson observation: guidance (DfEE 2000e)

		Lesson Observation: Time/Events Log	
		(If used, this should be completed during the lesson)	
		Date: **Teacher:** **Sheet No:**	
		Lesson: **Observer:**	

Time	Activity code	Description of activities in the classroom	Aspect

Suggested activity code

1 = Whole class interactive (teacher directed)   5 = Classroom management

2 = Whole class lecture   6 = Testing/assessment

3 = Individual work   7 = Transition between activities

4 = Collaborative work

Figure 5.7 Lesson observation: time/events log (DfEE 2000e)

Lesson Observation Sheet with prompts for looking at children				
Observer:		Observation started _____ ended _____		
Teacher: **Date:** **Year group:**				
Subject and learning objective:				
Prompts	**HA**	**AA**	**LA**	**Comments and evidence** **What impact does the teaching have on the pupils?**
Comply with ground rules Pay attention Behave well Relate well to adults and pupils Are interested Understand what they are to do Understand why they are doing an activity Gain new knowledge, skills Speak and listen well Errors corrected Work hard Act responsibly Understand how well they have done Understand how they can improve Praised for work				
Time: Pupils on task: _____ off task: _____				
Time: Pupils on task: _____ off task: _____				

© Bubb and Hoare 2001

Figure 5.8 Lesson Observation Sheet with prompts for looking at children

Lesson Observation Sheet with prompts for looking at teaching		
Observer:	**Observation started** _____ **ended** _____	
Teacher:		
Date:		
Year group:		
Subject and learning objective		
Prompts	**OK?**	**Comments and evidence** **What impact does the teaching have on the pupils?**
Ground rules		
Praises good behaviour and work		
Redirects off-task behaviour		
Consequences for poor behaviour		
High expectations		
Organised		
Resources		
Shares learning objectives		
Subject knowledge		
Relates new learning to old		
Explanations		
Deals with misunderstandings		
Voice – tone, volume		
Pace		
Use of time		
Questioning		
Motivating		
Differentiation		
Additional adults		
Feedback to children		
Suitable activities		
Plenary		
Time: Pupils on task: _____ off task: _____		
Time: Pupils on task: _____ off task: _____		

Figure 5.9 Lesson observation sheet with prompts for looking at teaching

Lesson Observation Sheet with prompts (blank)		
Observer:	Observation started _____ ended _____	
Teacher:		
Date:		
Year group:		
Subject and learning objective		
Prompts	**OK?**	**Comments and evidence** **What impact does the teaching have on the pupils?**
Time: Pupils on task: _____ off task: _____		
Time: Pupils on task: _____ off task: _____		

Figure 5.10 Lesson observation sheet with prompts (blank)

Classroom Observation Form
Teacher: **Subject,** **date and time:**
Observer:
Learning objective:
Additional adults:
Focus of observation:
Planning
Teaching
Class management

© Bubb and Hoare 2001

Figure 5.11 Observation Form with headings

Summary of Classroom Observation
Teacher:
Subject, date and time:
Observer:
Focus of observation:
Strengths of the lesson
Areas for further development
Objectives
Teacher's signature   Observer's signature

© Bubb and Hoare 2001

Figure 5.12 Strengths and Weaknesses Form

During the observation

1. Read the lesson plan, paying particular attention to the learning objective. Is it a sensible objective, and is it shared with the children? If you have a photocopy it is useful to annotate the plan, for instance showing what parts went well, when pace slowed, and so forth. Look at the teacher's planning file and children's work to see what the lesson is building on.

2. If the teacher has not given you a place to sit, choose one which is outside the direct line of the teacher's vision, but where you can see the children and what the teacher is doing. When the children are doing activities, move around to ascertain the effectiveness of the teacher's explanation, organisation and choice of task. Look at different groups (girls and boys; high, average and low attainers; and children with English as an additional language or special needs) to see whether everyone's needs are being met.

3. Make notes about what actually happens, focusing on the agreed areas but keeping your eyes open to everything. Make clear judgements as you gather evidence. Refer to the criteria you agreed to use – have a copy with you.

4. Try to tell 'the story' of the lesson, by noting causes and effect. For instance, what was it about the teacher's delivery that caused children's rapt attention or fidgeting?

5. Think about the pupils' learning and what it is about the teaching that is helping or hindering it. Note what children actually achieve. Teachers are not always aware that some children have only managed to write the date and that others have exceeded expectations, for instance. Look through children's books to get a feel for their progress and the teacher's marking.

6. Avoid teaching the children yourself or interfering in any way. This is very tempting! Children will often expect you to help them with spellings, for instance, but once you help one others will ask. This will distract you from your central purpose which is to observe the teaching and learning. It is not wise to intervene in controlling the class unless things get out of hand, because it can undermine the teachers' confidence and may confuse the children, who will see you as the one in charge rather than their teacher. As far as possible be unobtrusive.

7. Remember that as an established member of staff your presence will normally have an effect on the pupils – they will often be better behaved but sometimes show off. It is sometimes useful to leave the room for five minutes and loiter nearby to see if the noise level rises when you are not there and to get a feel for the atmosphere as you go back in. This can also be used when the lesson is going badly because it gives the teacher the opportunity to pull the class together.

8. Look friendly and positive throughout, even (and especially) if things are not going well. Say something positive to the teacher as you leave the class. Ideally, give an indication that you were pleased with what you saw. The teacher will be very anxious, and will almost always think the worst unless reassured.

After the observation

Reflect

Take some time to reflect. Think about the teaching and learning you have seen, focusing on strengths and a few areas for development. Use the format in Figure 6.2 for writing points to share with the teacher. Be clear about your main message – this will take some thinking about. There is no point listing every little thing that went wrong. You need to have 'the big picture' in your mind in order to convey it to the teacher. Remember it needs to be useful to them – aim to help them develop. You want to avoid the extremes of crushing them or giving the impression that things are better than they really are. It is a very fine line to tread, but your knowledge of the context and the teacher will help you.

Physical setting

Attend to the physical setting of the discussion. Choose a place where you will not be disturbed – you never know how someone is going to react in a feedback. Position chairs at right angles to each other for the most conducive atmosphere. This enables you to have eye contact but not in the formal direct way that sitting opposite someone across a desk would ensure. However, there will be times when such a setting will help you get a tough message across. A cup of coffee and biscuits can be a useful ice-breaker and shows that you value the teacher.

General tips

Be aware of your body language and notice the teacher's. A large proportion of communication is non-verbal, so:

– lean slightly forward
– uncross arms
– try to ignore any of your distracting inner thoughts
– make eye contact
– smile and nod
– listen actively.

Try to ask questions to guide their thinking, but not in a way that intimidates or implies criticism. Encourage reflection and listen well by asking open-ended questions, such as:

– How do you think the lesson went?
– What were you most pleased with? Why?
– What were you trying to achieve?
– What did the pupils learn?
– What did the lower attaining pupils learn?
– What did the higher attaining pupils learn?
– Why do you think the lesson went the way it did?
– Why did you choose that activity?
– Were there any surprises?
– When you did . . . . . . the pupils reacted by . . . . . . Why do you think that happened?

- Help me understand what you took into account when you were planning?
- If you taught that lesson again, what, if anything, would you do differently?
- What will you do in the follow up lesson?

Be aware of what you say, and how you say it. Focus on the teaching and learning that took place, using specific examples of what children said and did.

Avoid talking about yourself or other teachers you have seen unless this will be useful to the teacher. Comments such as 'I wouldn't have done that' or 'I would have . . .' are inappropriate (DfEE 2000f) and can irritate and alienate the teacher. It is sometimes tempting to talk about your most awful lesson. This can be comforting for the teacher, but can detract from the purpose of the discussion. Aim for the teacher to do most of the talking and thinking

Paraphrase and summarise what the teacher says. This helps the team leader concentrate on what is being said and is very helpful in getting a clear shared understanding of what the teacher thinks. It involves reflecting back your interpretation of what you have heard, which can be very useful for the teacher. Use phrases such as 'So what you mean is . . .', 'In other words . . .'.

Be positive and upbeat throughout. Sandwich potentially negative comments between positive ones. Be sensitive to how the teacher is taking your feedback, and ease off if necessary.

A framework for the post-observation discussion

It is useful to have some sort of structure for the post-lesson observation discussion. You need to use time well, feel in control of the situation and know where you want to get to. A common feedback structure is shown in Figure 5.13. I have found this of most use with students on teaching practice. However, the style of the structure tends towards the teacher being passive, listening to what the observer has to say. This is not always the best way to encourage someone to develop professionally. This should be done by encouraging the teacher to play a more active part and engage in a dialogue.

Improved framework for a post-observation discussion

Malderez and Bodoczky (1999, p.202) suggest using a framework for feedback that has different styles and actions in each of the phases. I have adapted their framework (see Figure 5.14) to lead into setting objectives and to end on a positive note by discussing the teacher's strengths. I have found that this helps the observer stay focused on the main points. It stops one going round in circles or going off at unhelpful tangents. This is how the phases work.

Pre-phase 1 – Decide on key points
It is important to go into a post-observation discussion with a clear view of what you think are the teacher's strengths, and more importantly what you think they need to work on to be even more effective. Make a list of the 'weaknesses' of the lesson. Decide which ones impacted most on the children's progress and well-being. This should stop you raising points which are simply your own idiosyncratic feelings. For

Phase	Commentary
1. Observer asks teacher 'How do you think the lesson went?'	Teacher does not know what the observer's judgement is, so may be cagey not wanting to be a hostage to fortune. Some teachers say little ('it was OK') and others say too much. Some have exactly the same view of the lesson as you which makes things easier for you. Others will think the lesson successful when you had misgivings, but more often people just focus on the things that did not go well. Either way, this gives you an insight into how they think, which will determine how you develop the feedback. If they think they are better than you think they are you may have to be tougher in your message. If they are over self-critical, you need to boost them up. Some people go off at a tangent that after ten minutes leaves you utterly confused. For example, they might say, 'Well, it wasn't one of my best. I was going to plan it in lots of detail last night but the bus was late and got held up in traffic. Then when I got off I realised that I'd left my umbrella on it so . . . and then . . . and then . . . and then . . . etc.' I think that some people do this deliberately to deflect attention!
2a. Observer either: goes over their notes chronologically with strengths and weaknesses mingled; or	This gives a detailed picture of the lesson, but overall may not give a clear message about what was good and what needs to be improved.
2b. Outlines strengths and successes and then areas to develop.	Strengths and areas for development are clear, but the teacher may not pay attention to what you liked because they are waiting for the 'but', the negatives. In both 2a and 2b the teacher is inclined to be passive while you feedback, unless you ask questions.
3a. 'So I think these are your action points?'; or	This gives the teacher no active role in deciding what needs to be worked on. They may act on your suggestions successfully but often they do not because they do not feel ownership of them.
3b. 'What do you think you need to work on?'	This gives the teacher some choice in prioritising what the observer thinks they need to do, but responsibility is minimal.

© Bubb and Hoare 2001

Figure 5.13 A typical feedback structure

instance, some people will feel irritated by things such as the teacher pacing up and down, punctuating every sentence with 'er', or speaking in a monotone, but these should not be raised unless they are affecting the children's learning. You should also consider whether the teacher will be able to change or improve – things like voice and mannerisms are very hard to alter. You could plan main points using a format such as the one in Figure 5.15.

Phase 1 – Warm up

Thank the teacher for letting you observe. Give a brief headline of what you thought of the lesson – this is what they want to know. If it went well, say so. If it went badly, say something reassuring but that does not mislead them. Commenting on the children or the subject matter of the lesson can be useful:

– 'Thank you for letting me observe. What a lively class you've got!'
– 'Thank you for letting me observe. Speech marks are really difficult to teach.'
– 'Thank you for letting me observe. Why do children get so wound up by the wind?'
– 'Thank you for letting me observe. I found it very interesting.'
– 'Thank you for letting me observe. There are some issues I think we need to discuss.'

Phase 2 – Teacher's views

Ask the teacher how they thought it went, and why. This will give you an insight into how they evaluate their work. Some have exactly the same view of the lesson as you, which makes things easier. Others will think the lesson successful when you had misgivings, but more often people focus on the things that did not go well. Either way, this gives you an insight into how they think, which will determine how you develop the feedback. If they think they are better than you think, they are, consider their reasoning – they might be right. If after listening you really feel that their needs are even greater you may have to be tougher in your message. If they are overly self-critical, you need to boost them up.

Phase 3 – Leading factual statement

Having gained more information about the teacher, you need to quickly decide on what you think are the most important things to address. Link these to the affects they are having on the children. A useful strategy is to use factual statements (Malderez and Bodoczky 1999) about what you heard or saw, without including a judgement. So, if you think the pace was rather slow in the plenary you could say, 'I saw three children yawn during the plenary.' The teacher can offer their reason for the behaviour. This might be any of the following:

'Yes, I agree. I think the way I do plenaries – asking a group to read out their work – is a bit boring.'
'Hmm, I think I ran out of steam by then.'
'Yes, those three were up late watching the football match on TV.'
'It was rather hot in the room.'

This enables them to think of explanations, and probably solutions.

However, if you interpret what was seen, 'I saw three children looking bored', your interpretation, the children were bored, may actually be wrong. Even if your interpretation is right, the teacher is immediately put on the defensive and is unlikely to open up and reflect in a confident way.

Phase 4 – Probes

The next phase leads naturally on from the last. You will need to probe further, asking questions that guide the teacher's thinking more deeply about a particular issue. If they give straightforward reasons that you agree with you can move to the next phase: thinking about alternatives. Probing questions will occur to you *in situ* but generally they will be 'why' ones such as 'Why do you think that is?' You can then move into the 'how' phase.

Phase 5 – Alternatives

When you are in this phase the teacher and you should be discussing alternatives: how to make a specific aspect of their teaching more effective. A key question would be 'How else might you . . .?' Ideally the teacher should think up their own solutions, but you can suggest some too. See your role as someone who allows the teacher to reflect off, and who asks the questions that encourage them to think of the solutions themselves.

Phase 6 – Objectives

You can then raise the status of the discussion by phrasing the action points as written objectives. Think of what things should happen, by whom, with what help and by when. Write these as you would any other objective.

Phase 7 – Strengths

Having got the areas for development out of the way you can now have a relaxed discussion which will feature you telling the teacher in detail about their strengths and the successes of the lesson as you see them. This will be a boost to the teacher, and lead them to feel confident and ready to implement the areas for development. Make sure you do not mention these again, so that your last words are about the many things that they do well. Do not be afraid to use fulsome praise, linking their teaching to the progress and well-being of the children.

Using the framework in Figure 5.15, against each of the phases make notes about what you might say about an observation. Having rehearsed this mentally, try using the framework in a post-observation discussion. It takes practice, but people attending my courses have found it very useful. People that I have used this with in feeding back to also feel that they were more active, reflective and boosted by it. It also seems to take a shorter time than other feedback structures.

The next chapter contains ideas for monitoring planning and setting objectives for specific problems that teachers may encounter.

Framework for post-observation discussion			
Phase	Team leader prompt	Team leader action	Teacher action
Pre 1. Key points		Be clear about strengths and what you think should be improved.	
1. Warm up and headline	'Thank you for letting me observe. That was a good lesson.'	Gives brief, positive overall comment to set tone.	Listens. Hears headline of what you thought.
2. Teacher's view of the lesson	'How do you think it went?' 'Talk me through . . .'	Listens actively, analysing teacher reflection and mentally deciding how to play the rest of the discussion.	Describes their view of the lesson.
3. Leading factual statement	'I noticed . . .'	Describes with a purpose.	Listens and interprets.
4. Probes	'Why do you think that was?'	Probes.	Considers reasons and reflects more deeply.
5. Alternatives	'How else could you . . .?' 'Why don't you . . .?'	Leads the teacher to thinking of solutions or improvements. Makes suggestions.	Considers other ways of doing things.
6. Objectives	'What objectives and actions would help you?'	Helps think of objectives and writes them down.	Thinks of objectives and actions.
7. Strengths	'I now want to talk about the strengths of the lesson . . .'	Summarises, reaffirming strengths, successes and progress.	Listens and feels good.

© Bubb and Hoare 2001

Figure 5.14 Framework for a post-observation discussion that leads into setting objectives

Framework for planning post-observation discussion	
Phase	**Planning notes**
Pre 1. Key points	
1. Warm up and headline	
2. Teacher's view of the lesson	
3. Leading factual statement	
4. Probes	
5. Alternatives	
6. Objectives	
7. Strengths	

© Bubb and Hoare 2001

Figure 5.15 Framework for a planning a post-observation discussion

6 Monitoring planning

The monitoring of planning

There has been much change in the expectations of teacher planning since the introduction of the Literacy and Numeracy Strategies. The content and longitudinal structure of planning – the long- and medium-term elements – have been largely covered in these documents. The QCA schemes of work, where schools have elected to use them, have performed much the same role for the remaining subjects. It is, however, worthwhile revisiting the basic principle of planning, since some teachers, particularly those who have qualified recently, may not be aware of the interlinking aspects of the different levels of planning.

Planning ultimately derives from the needs of the children and the aims that the school has for them. Thus the school philosophy provides the starting point for planning. Long-term planning will include aspects that link directly to the school philosophy and usually on a one or two year cycle. It will contain reference to both strategies, the National Curriculum Programmes of Study, Foundation Stage Guidance and the QCA schemes of work. Medium-term planning covers a term or half term and provides the next layer of detail. Short-term planning is weekly and covers what children will do every day. Good examples of planning may be found in the wide range of documents associated with the Strategies, and on the Virtual Teachers Centre on the DfEE website (www.dfee.gov.uk).

Each school will develop its own approach to planning and its own criteria defining what constitutes satisfactory planning. This will vary from school to school because the children will have different needs; it will also vary because the skills, experience and understanding of the teachers themselves will also vary. All teachers need to be clear about what planning is expected of them, and the extent and standard of planning.

Tips for monitoring planning
- Decide on a focus, subject and time span (a month or term's worth of planning?).
- Collect all the planning that you need in one place.
- Make clear to teachers what you require so that they provide what you need.
- Set a time limit for the monitoring – and stick to it! If the job takes too long perhaps your focus needs to be more specific.
- Note down your judgements, using a format such as the one in Figure 6.1. However, you could write your own prompts (see Figure 3.1).

Prompts	Comments
Is the planning organised suitably in a file?	
Do the plans cover the appropriate parts of the curriculum?	
Is the teacher following the school planning policies and practices?	
Is the teacher following the school schemes of work and long-term plans?	
Can you track work through long-, medium- and short-term plans?	
Are useful links made between subjects, to aid children's learning?	
Does the planning cover the same work as parallel classes?	
Does the planning show appropriate expectations?	
Is the right amount of work being planned for the time allocation?	
Has the teacher drawn up a suitable timetable for when different work is to be done?	
Are learning intentions clear?	
Are there different learning objectives and/or activities to allow children of different attainment to progress?	
Does the planning take into account the needs of pupils not yet fluent in English?	
Do the activities enable objectives to be met?	
Are the resources and activities appropriate and interesting?	
Are there planned assessment opportunities?	
Are plans informed by assessing children's knowledge, skills and understanding?	
Are lessons evaluated?	

© Bubb and Hoare 2001

Figure 6.1 Monitoring a teacher's planning

Addressing problems in planning

There are common problems in planning. Frequently experienced problems include those that stem from weak subject knowledge.

Subject knowledge

This is an area that all teachers find an issue. The number of changes, new strategies and developments mean that everyone is constantly having to deal with new parts of the curriculum. Changing year groups and key stages increases the amount of subject knowledge needed.

New teachers have had a comparatively short amount of time to gain a great deal of knowledge, especially if they trained on the PGCE which is a one year course. Some will come with greater knowledge of the most up-to-date thinking on some subjects than experienced colleagues. Others will have gaps in their knowledge because their course was not able to give some subjects much attention. The QTS standards (DfEE 1998b, see Appendix) are focused on English, mathematics, science and ICT, which gives little time for anything else. The age range and subjects covered in teaching practices will vary. Many teachers will be teaching year groups that they did not teach on their final practice. Some may be teaching in a different key stage and so will need even greater help in getting to grips with the curriculum.

Pedagogy is also very important. Teachers need to know how children of different ages learn best, and to teach accordingly. One of the hardest things I have done in my career was to take a reception class after teaching Year 6 for several years.

With all issues relating to subject knowledge it is essential to diagnose the problem accurately. This is best done by asking the teacher to evaluate their strengths and weaknesses. This can be the focus of discussion. A programme of support and monitoring could include:

– self study – working through the National Literacy Strategy materials, for instance;
– planning partners;
– staff meetings;
– courses;
– discussion with subject coordinators; and
– observation of other teachers.

Planning

Problems with planning have a very detrimental effect on all other areas of the standards. Many, but not all, are to do with insecure subject and pedagogical knowledge. Some are to do with the teaching strategies used. Here are some different types of problem that teachers may have with planning.

Types of problems with planning
1. Used to using different formats.
2. Needing to do more detailed planning than other teachers.
3. Doing too little planning.
4. Doing too much planning – and getting exhausted.

5. Imprecise learning objectives.
6. Activities not matching learning objectives.
7. Insufficiently high expectations.
8. Insufficient differentiation.
9. Not covering enough of the curriculum at sufficient depth.
10. Over-reliance on commercial schemes or other people's ideas.
11. Uses the activities suggested in team planning but does not think about how to do them.
12. Does not stick to year group plans.
13. Planning looks good on paper but the children do not make progress.
14. Weak parts of a generally satisfactory plan.

Case Studies – problems with planning

The following case studies illustrate different types of problems with planning – and possible remedies through objective-setting.

1. Used to using different planning formats

Emma is confused by the different expectations and formats used by her previous and present school. She is not comfortable with the school's formats and finds most boxes too small. She ends up using the school formats to keep the head teacher happy but uses her own more detailed ones as well. In effect she is duplicating work.

Objective
To use just the school's formats for planning by half term.

Action
Make the school's planning expectations and the reasoning behind them absolutely clear to Emma, using other teachers' work as examples. Ask her to talk through the differences between the school's and teaching practice planning formats. Does she have a point about the school's formats – are they as useful as they could be? Hopefully the discussion will enable Emma to see that the difference between the formats is fairly cosmetic.

Give feedback on the teacher's planning, showing how she can avoid duplication and where she can cut down the amount of writing. Make sure that she knows that it is perfectly all right to do extra planning where she feels it is necessary.

2. Needing to do more detailed planning than other teachers

Carol was used to doing more detailed written planning than experienced teachers in her school. For instance, her school only required that the teachers plan their literacy hours on a weekly A3 sheet, whereas Carol had been used to writing a detailed lesson plan for each literacy hour. She felt that she should only use the A3 sheet and thought that there must be something wrong with her because she needed much more detail for the lesson to go well.

Objective
To reduce the time spent planning to x hours a week.

Action

Make sure that Carol understands the school's expectations for her planning, which are that she only needs to do what everyone else does but that when she needs to write in more detail she should. Ask her to keep a record of how long she plans for in a week, and try to reduce it gradually.

Boost her self-confidence by giving feedback on Carol's planning, preferably having seen a plan being taught. Identify where corners could be cut in writing her plans.

3. Doing too little planning

Simon reacted against the stringent demands of the induction year by doing too little planning, particularly because he did not have to show it to the head teacher. After an observation of a disastrous lesson his team leader asked to see the lesson plan. He pulled from his pocket an old envelope with some notes scribbled on it.

Objective

Plan teaching in accordance with school policy.

Action

Make planning expectations clear, using other teachers' work as examples.

Help Simon to see that lessons go better and children learn more when they are well planned.

Ensure that all planning is given to the head teacher at the beginning of every week, and returned if it lacks detail.

4. Doing too much planning – and getting exhausted

Kate found it hard not to plan at teaching practice level. She soon filled lever arch files with reams of paper and found that she was spending every waking hour planning and revising lessons. Although she handed weekly plans to the head teacher, she received no feedback on them. On teaching practice her plans were looked at in detail and commented upon regularly, and she found herself missing this. Inevitably she burnt out.

Objective

To reduce the time spent planning to x hours a week.

Action

The head teacher to give feedback on planning. This will provide a much needed boost to Kate's confidence. Ask her to keep a record of how long she plans for in a week, and try to reduce it gradually. Identify where corners could be cut in writing her plans.

5. Imprecise learning objectives

Kevin wrote learning objectives on plans but they were insufficiently focused on what the children would be able to do by the end of the lesson. Here are a selection:

Characteristic features of a period

Instruction text – dissolving

What is an atlas?

To try to understand the idea of friendship

He did not break them down in to smaller units. As a result the children seemed to be doing activities rather than learning.

Objective
For all learning objectives to be so clear that they can be shared with children.

Action
Show Kevin how the learning objectives in other people's planning are phrased and arrange for him to observe a teacher who explains the lesson's objectives to the children. Monitor plans and give feedback, emphasising the learning objectives.

6. Activities not matching learning objectives

Beth did not think carefully enough about whether the activities she did with her Year 3 class were the best way of meeting her learning objectives. For instance, for the National Literacy Strategy (NLS) objective 'to discuss characters' feelings, behaviour and relationships, referring to the text' she chose to use *Mr Men* books. (For those of you not familiar with these books, they are popular with pre-school children and about characters such as Mr Grumpy and Mr Noisy. These people have one dimensional characters – not quite what the authors of the NLS were intending!)

Objective
To deepen understanding of literacy.

To plan activities that enable children to meet the learning objectives.

Action
Discuss planning with the English coordinator, and perhaps read some books with ideas for Year 3 literacy. To evaluate children's learning against the learning objective to decide whether the activity enabled them to meet it.

7. Insufficiently high expectations

Maureen worked in an inner city reception class with a high proportion of very needy children. She loved and cared for them well, but her planning showed low expectations. She planned few formal class or group sessions and lots of free choice. In the taught group sessions objectives were often too easy. For instance, children were asked to count up to 10 objects when they could have gone over 20. The class often misbehaved because they were insufficiently occupied.

Objective
To have high but realistic expectations of her class and plan accordingly.

Action
Arrange for Maureen to visit some other reception classes with children of similar backgrounds to see what can be achieved. She could also look at the work that the Year 1 class are doing to see where her children need to be in a year's time. If she spent some time finding out what her pupils can already do, she could plan activities that move them on.

8. Insufficient differentiation

Nick's planning met the needs of the majority of the class well but he did not cater for those who found learning difficult or those who were very able. Thus, in every lesson there were children off task because they were bored or worried, either because the activity was too easy or impossibly hard.

Objective
To differentiate activities so that the high attainers are challenged and the low attainers can make progress.

Action
Nick needs to assess the high and low attainers to discover what they can and cannot do, and then plan to meet their needs. His learning objectives could be differentiated by distinguishing between what all, some and a few children will achieve by the end of the lesson. He can differentiate the activities by outcome, task or the level of support. Looking at someone else's planning and teaching will help.

9. Not covering enough of the curriculum at sufficient depth

Pam felt worried about gaps in her own knowledge of science. She had only a vague understanding of the concepts in the school's scheme of work for forces at Year 6. She did not have the time or resources to improve her understanding by reading. Instead she resorted to giving the children commercial worksheets and often her science lessons were very brief.

Objective
To identify and address areas of weakness in her subject knowledge of forces.
To plan work that will cover the science curriculum in adequate depth for Year 6.

Action
Pam needs to identify what she does not understand about forces and then read some books to improve her knowledge. Children's books are often good at explaining concepts clearly. She should use ideas from the science coordinator and books to plan activities that aid children's learning.

10. Over-reliance on commercial schemes or other people's ideas

Naseem felt very insecure. She planned with the other Year 4 teachers, who were very experienced and appeared much more knowledgeable than her. Overawed, she contributed little to the planning meetings and used all the others' ideas. Her lessons rarely seemed to go as well as her colleagues. She was also over-reliant on activities and worksheets from commercial schemes rather than thinking of the needs of the individuals in her class.

Objective
To take a more active part at planning meetings, and plan some lessons for the rest of the team.

Action
Naseem needs to be more confident in planning. To help her, one would have to ascertain the reason for her lack of confidence. Is it because of weak subject knowledge?

She needs to be directed to some useful teachers' resource books to get ideas for planning and then to think how activities could be used with her class. Her planning partners could encourage her ideas more and ask her to plan certain lessons. She should be encouraged to think not just of what the children are going to do, and why, but how and when.

11. Uses the activities suggested in team planning but does not think about how to do them

James followed the team planning in which he played an active part. He was confused when his lessons were deemed unsatisfactory by an OFSTED inspector who had given a very good grade to his colleague teaching the very same lesson. James was not used to thinking carefully about how to explain the learning objectives to the children and his input during the lesson was not as thorough or motivating as his colleagues. His class made less progress than the parallel classes during the year.

Objective

To plan in more depth, thinking about how to explain things to children to maximise their learning.

Action

James needs to see his colleagues in the parallel classes teach a lesson that he has taught to his class. He should reflect on the similarities and differences between his delivery and theirs, and put what he learns into practice.

12. Does not stick to year group plans

Kit was a very extrovert creative person who did not like being constrained by team planning. She would often change the activity that had been jointly decided, because she had thought of a more fun one. The children loved their teacher, enjoyed every lesson and learned a great deal. One of them, however, had a twin sister in the parallel class whose parents complained that their children were having very different experiences at school, which they felt was an equal opportunities issue.

Objective

To understand the importance of joint planning and the need to share ideas that improve on the original planning.

Action

While one does not want to inhibit her creativity, Kit needs to realise that planning is done jointly to give children in the same year group similar experiences. She should be encouraged to share her good ideas with colleagues in the parallel classes so that they can decide whether they should all change the activities.

13. Planning looks good on paper but the children do not make enough progress

Prema kept a meticulous planning file and all her work was word-processed. It looked very good, but her children did not make as much progress as in the previous year. When observed, her induction tutor found that her teaching strategies and explanations were not being effective.

Objective
To assess what children learn and the progress they make.

To improve teaching strategies and explanations.

Action
Prema needs to understand that her children could be making better progress. She could observe another teacher using her plan with her class to see the different strategies and explanations they use.

14. Weak parts of a generally satisfactory plan

Richard planned most of his lessons very well. It was only when his teaching was observed that people realised he was not planning plenaries. The children were not being reminded about the original learning objectives and were not asked to judge how well they had met them. Learning was not drawn together and lessons just fizzled out.

Objective
To plan and execute plenaries in all lessons.

Action
Richard should be praised for his good planning, but reminded of the value of plenaries. He could observe another teacher's plenary and look at how it was planned. His plenaries should always refer to the original learning objective and children should be able to say how well they met them.

Planning for additional adults

Many classes have additional adults to support pupils with SEN, EAL, literacy and numeracy. Most are high quality, but some can prove to be a management issue. Here are some problems identified by teachers:

- Being unsure of the additional adult's role.
- Not sure when they are going to be in the class.
- Not knowing what to ask them to do.
- Not wanting to ask them to do menial tasks.
- Some do too much for the children and encourage over-dependence.
- Some have poor grammar and spelling and so cannot help the children.
- Some have little control over the children.
- Some can take over the class.

– Some talk when the teacher has asked for everyone's attention.
– Some are stuck in their ways and do not like new ideas and practices.
– Finding time to talk to them to explain the activity.
– Planning for them, but they do not turn up.

It is very hard for teachers to find time to talk to other adults who are working in the class. This often means that they are not used to best effect because the teacher needs to explain the activity and what they should do. A plan that can be given to them at an appropriate time should help this situation (see Figure 6.2).

Teachers should think about what they want the other adult to do during the whole-class teaching parts of the lesson. This could be a time to prepare resources or for them to be involved with certain children, checking their understanding for instance. Additional adults will want to know which children to support and where they should work. Most importantly, they need to know what the children should do, what they should do to help them and what the children should learn. Giving the adult a list of resources that they will need means that they can be responsible for getting them out.

Additional adults have important information about the children they work with. They often know more about children with special needs, for instance, than the class teacher. These insights can be tapped by asking the adult to make some notes about how the children got on.

In the next chapter we shall look at ways to monitor children's work and teachers' assessments.

Plan for additional adult

Name: **Lesson and time:**

What to do while I am whole-class teaching:

   Introduction   Plenary

Children to support: **Where and when:**

Activity:

   What the children should do:

   What I would like you to do:

   What I want them to get out of it:

   Things that they will need:

How did they get on?

Thank you!

Figure 6.2 Plan for an additional adult in the classroom

7 Monitoring children's work and teacher's assessment

Work samples

To carry out a work sampling exercise it is essential to develop an overall marking policy and ensure that it is followed for each year group. Many schools differentiate their marking policy across the age ranges. It is also helpful to carry out periodic exercises with a member of the management team leading a review, which is either subject or year group based.

The most common way to construct a work sample is for the coordinator to agree with the class teacher on a sample of pupils whose work will be looked at on a regular basis. The OFSTED system of looking at the work of a high, average and below average attainer is convenient and will provide useful evidence for the next inspection, when it can be used to demonstrate the school's approach to assessment as well as monitoring standards in particular subjects. Having chosen an able, an average and a below average child, the coordinator and the class teacher can agree on a longitudinal focus for sampling. It would be sensible to look at areas identified in the school development plan for the particular subject for example. The coordinator will need to have copies of the planning relating to the particular lesson, and will need to make a judgement about how well the teaching promoted the aims of the lesson as shown through the pupils' work. Due allowance will of course be made for different abilities, and looking at how the teacher differentiated work for each child and how successful this was will be key areas. (See Figure 7.1.)

An important part of the evaluation of a work sample is the observations relating to marking. It is important to make sure that teachers have a clear understanding that what is needed from marking is clear instruction for the pupil on how to improve in future. This is why it is important to consider the learning objectives and the assessment indicators. Were the children aware of what constituted success?

A marking exercise can be done as a variation on the familiar moderation of levels exercise, where a work focus is chosen and staff consider which National Curriculum level to assign to particular pieces of work. The following checklists can be adapted for use in different year groups and with tasks from different curriculum areas.

The criteria for the standards expected must be carefully discussed and will often match the learning objectives set for the task. For example:

Possible context for lower Key Stage 2
   Plan and write a poem which uses strong verbs and appropriate adjectives.
   Plan a story using a framework. Make sure your framework is really usable.
   Organise a complete piece of writing using headings, layout and instructions. Use correct grammar, punctuation and the impersonal style.

Child's name:	**Class/Year group:**
Date of birth:	**IEP/IAP:**
Date/Time taken:	
Curriculum area:	

Learning objectives set by teacher
Assessment indicators identified by teacher
Does the work done match the learning objectives?
Is it at the appropriate level?

Figure 7.1 Monitoring of a sample of work

Possible context for upper Key Stage 2
>Write a story with a maximum of four characters, a setting, two problems and a resolution. Include dialogue, description and action.
>Plan a piece of writing which uses one of the frameworks we have been studying and use a plan to produce a completed piece of text.

Once the learning objectives and the context are agreed work can begin on the marking criteria, which is often helpfully laid out as a checklist. One might specify a certain number of headings for the plan, four for example: the use of a dictionary or thesaurus; inclusion of capitals and full stops; the required level of sophistication of verbs and adjectives; sequencing of ideas; rhythm; creative ideas. It is also helpful to give teachers an understanding of how much time might be required. In the possible context for lower Key Stage 2, one might need one lesson to revise the planning of a poem, two lessons to write out the plan and the poem within the context of the group level work perhaps.

Marking checklist – an example for upper KS2

Excellent/Better than expected/Meets all criteria/Good/As expected
  Three out of four headings used
  Four words or ideas under each heading
  Powerful verbs under three of the four headings
  Adjectives generally match subject matter
  Sensible choices made: sensible poem, sensible sequence
  Not too repetitious
  Some sense of rhythm
  Common words spelt correctly
  Difficult words phonetically plausible
  Capital letter and full stops correct

Insufficient progress/Slightly disappointing
  Two out of four headings in correct place
  Two/three words or ideas, mostly appropriate, under each heading
  Some powerful verbs match subject
  Some suitable adjectives
  Some sensible choices
  Some ideas related to each other
  Two/three examples of sense of rhythm
  More than half common words spelt correctly
  Some capitals, full stops correct

Low level/Much less than expected
  Vague attempt made to plan
  Some input discernible (e.g. words under wrong heading)
  Little knowledge of a range of verbs
  Little knowledge of a range of adjectives
  Little evidence of plan being used
  No sequence
  No rhythm
  Few words spelt accurately
  Little punctuation

Looking at children's books

Children's work is a useful source of evidence about the effectiveness of an teacher. It is in many ways the proof of the pudding. Again, it is easier to select the work of a few children of different levels of attainment rather than look at the whole class. Figure 7.2 can be used to sample work, though you may prefer to write prompts relating to your specific focus using Figure 3.1. Figures 7.3 and 7.4 would be useful in monitoring numeracy and literacy across the whole curriculum.

Tips

- Have a focus and time limit. Looking at children's books can be very time-consuming so you need to have a clear focus and a time limit of say one hour in total.

- Look at a high, average and low attainer.
- Compare recent and old work. This will give you a feel for progress.
- Look at plans to check learning objectives and the context of the work.
- Have level descriptions to hand so that you can judge attainment against national standards.
- Compare three children's work on a certain date. This will show you how the teacher has catered for different needs.
- Note down hunches. Too often these are just in your head. Write them down, then talk to the teacher and use the evidence to test your hypotheses.

Assessment

Analysing a teacher's planning and assessments can be very difficult, especially if they teach a year group that you are not experienced in. It is best done by the year or phase group coordinator, if the school has one; and with the teacher so that they can explain where evidence lies.

Summative and ongoing formative assessments will probably be kept in different places, depending on the age of the children and the school's and teacher's systems. Places where evidence for assessment might be are:

Assessment folder	Guided writing records
Baseline assessments	Reading folder
Records of achievement	Home–school reading diary
Marking in children's exercise books	IEPs
Targets in children's exercise books	Behaviour book
Teacher's mark book	Significant achievement book
Lesson evaluations on plans	Letters to parents
Group reading records	Reports

Rather than looking at all the class, you might find looking at the assessments of just a few children useful. Choose a high, average and low attainer and a child with English as an additional language, for instance.

Monitoring through looking at marking

The key communication between teacher and pupil is through feedback on work. This may be communicated verbally or through comments on the work itself. However it is done, the school must develop ways of standardising this process so that teachers are giving it sufficient time, and so that it is useful to pupils. If they find the teacher's comments of no help, what is the point of the teacher making them? Why was the work set in the first place if its completion and marking do not lead directly and immediately to improvement of some aspect of the pupil's work?

When thinking about the marking policy, the following headings may be useful starting points.

Prompt	Comment
Does the children's work match the teacher's planning?	
Is there a balance of work, e.g. text, sentence and word level in literacy books?	
Is there evidence of the teacher's systems being used, e.g. date, title, handwriting conventions?	
Are school policies in use?	
What does the presentation tell you about the children's motivation and concentration?	
Are children doing enough work? Compare their output with a parallel class.	
Is the work differentiated?	
Is there enough challenge for low, average and high attainers so that all can make progress?	
Is there progress over time?	
What difference is there between work at the beginning and end of exercise books or folders?	
Is there any unnecessary repetition?	
Is the work marked in accordance with the school policy?	
Do children know how well they have met the objective of the work?	
Are children responding to the teacher's marking?	
Are errors corrected?	
What systems are there for dealing with repeated errors?	
Is there evidence that children are taking their targets into account?	

Figure 7.2 Sampling children's work

Subject	How numeracy promotes progress in these subjects	How the subject contributes to numeracy skills
EN		
SC		
ICT		
AR		
DT		
GG		
HI		
Mu		
PE		
RE		
Overall judgement		

© Bubb and Hoare 2001

Figure 7.3 Monitoring numeracy across the curriculum

Subject	Reading competence promotes progress	Writing competence promotes progress	How the subject contributes to literacy
Ma			
SC			
ICT			
AR			
DT			
GG			
HI			
Mu			
PE			
RE			
Overall judgement			

© Bubb and Hoare 2001

Figure 7.4 Monitoring literacy across the curriculum

Aims

These should define what the policy sets out to do, and why; and there should be clear links to the school ethos and mission statement.

The purposes of marking

Teachers should be able to read a clear statement about why work is marked. This should explain its role for pupils, parents, teaching staff. Links to other aspects of assessment, recording and reporting need to be made.

The principles underlying practice

Teachers often regard marking as a chore. The process of reviewing marking and developing a policy should emphasise its role in building best practice, in providing feedback, specificity and accuracy, developmental comments, pupil involvement and consistent practice.

The processes of marking

Teachers should be aware of the regularity of marking, the agreed marking code, marking and follow-up with pupils, the use of grades and scores and any other aspects it is agreed that the school will concentrate on.

The responsibilities

Everyone should know their responsibilities and that of others: the teachers as markers, the coordinator and others in a management role as monitors of policy and practice.

Recording and reporting

Your marking policy needs to reflect the ethos and nature of your school, but the following pointers may help you to ensure that important aspects are not left out. They can also be used to review your existing policy.

What should be in an assessment policy?

- Key principles – The reasons for assessment, what the aims are, how the school practice will help achievement of these aims.
- Statutory requirements – Brief notes on what has to be done. These often change so make sure you are up-to-date.
- Recording and reporting – What will be recorded in summative records and end of key stage records, who will receive them and when. How samples of work and records of achievement will contribute. The nature and form of reports to parents and pupils. Arrangements for consultation events and recording special needs (this will link to your SEN policy).
- Aspects of formative assessment – What teachers are expected to do, the range of assessment strategies, links to planning, the nature of records kept. Your marking policy can be included here or as an appendix.

- Pupils' involvement in assessment – The principles behind their involvement and details of what this means in practical terms for records of achievement, profiling and the marking of work.
- Developing consistency – Arrangements for moderating assessment judgements, agreement trialling and the production of portfolios of exemplar work.
- Using assessment data – How data will be used to evaluate group and school performance and the setting of targets; the role of governors in evaluation; the nature, timing and use of other school-based formal tests (i.e. NFER, reading, etc.).
- Roles and responsibilities – An outline of the responsibilities of senior managers, the assessment coordinator, heads of department, subject leaders and governors,
- Monitoring the policy – How practice will be reviewed, with guidance on responsibilities, strategies and frequency of activities. Dates.
- Links to other policies – Where particular aspects are developed further in other policies such as pastoral and subject policies, special needs and planning, etc.

Monitoring policy into practice

As always, the most difficult part of the process is the implementation and establishment of new approaches. It is worth considering a range of success criteria related to the aspects of monitoring considered so far. Having considered what constitutes good teaching and learning in your school, and shared this with the staff, you are in a position to take the next step, improvement in standards. First of all, though, make sure that the early stages are secure: consider whether your policy and practice encourage effective assessment, recording and reporting, if they do, what will result? Figure 7.5 can be used for getting an overall picture of whether the assessment policy is working in practice and Figure 7.6 can be used to get a picture of individual teachers' practice.

A similar format (Figure 7.7) can be used for monitoring marking. This is a key area, because it is at the heart of assessment: this is where the pupils get their messages about how they are doing, it is what forms their feelings about school. It is a foot in the door that leads to boosting self-esteem and developing positive motivation for teachers as well as pupils.

A similar approach is useful in relation to the end product of assessment, reports to parents. It is important to retain a sense of proportion: in many ways the pupils and their parents are the 'customers' of education, and the school's interactions with both these groups are of key importance. Hence the usefulness of success criteria for the monitoring of reports to parents (see Figure 7.8).

The first step is to debate what everyone in the school believes to be good teaching and learning and begin to move towards implementing these ideals. Next, a common understanding and expectation of assessment and its importance for motivating children and informing parents needs to be reached. Leading on from this, a sensible step might be to consider the nature of the records that need to be kept, such as:

- Do they include details of National Curriculum levels?
- Do they include other achievements made?
- Are they accessible and comprehensible?
- Are they completed in a planned way?

Success criteria	Comments
Teachers' plans are clear about learning outcomes	
Learning outcomes are shared with pupils	
Questioning and discussion are used well to assess progress	
Teachers have an agreed system for noting achievement	
Classroom assistants contribute to assessment practice	
Teachers use plenaries to review learning	
Pupils are involved in self-assessment	
Assessment is planned into teachers' work	
Assessment results in refining planning	
Pupils are clear about how they need to improve	
Teachers are confident in using a range of assessment strategies	
Practice conforms to the school policy	

© Bubb and Hoare 2001

Figure 7.5 Monitoring policy into practice

Prompts	Comments
Are assessments organised suitably?	
Are assessments covering appropriate parts of the curriculum?	
Is the teacher following the school's planning policies and practices?	
Are assessments analytical, rather than just descriptive?	
Is assessment information useful? Is it used to inform planning?	
Are pupils with SEN being monitored against their IEP targets?	
Are appropriate targets being set?	
Is progress towards the children's targets being monitored?	
Is the teacher accurate in judging the National Curriculum level of pieces of work?	
Are record-keeping systems efficient?	
Is marking up-to-date?	
Is work marked against the learning intention?	
Are pupils clear about how well they are doing?	
Do pupils know what to do to improve?	
Are literacy and numeracy errors highlighted in all subjects?	
Are reports well-written?	
Do reports give a clear picture of the child?	

© Bubb and Hoare 2001

Figure 7.6 Monitoring a teacher's assessment practices

Success criteria	Comments
Work is marked regularly	
Marking reflects learning outcomes	
Marking makes use of an agreed code	
Comments are supportive	
Comments say what needs to be improved	
Pupils correct their own work	
Pupils understand the marking system	
Parents understand the marking system	
Marking practice meets policy statements	
Marking practice is consistent	

© Bubb and Hoare 2001

Figure 7.7 Monitoring marking

Success criteria	Comments
Comments are clear and supportive	
Achievements are stated clearly	
National Curriculum levels are included for pupils at the end of key stages	
Next steps are emphasised	
Grades and levels are understood	

© Bubb and Hoare 2001

Figure 7.8 Monitoring reports to parents

- Do they show consistent practice?
- Do they comply with schools subject policies?
- Do they involve pupils in the process?

Where pupils are older, one may usefully ask them about assessment, recording and reporting. Some form of monitoring checklist, such as Figure 7.9, could indicate how far the school has come, and the extent of the task ahead. Some form of number ranking may be appropriate: for example, 1 Always, 2 Usually, 3 Sometimes, 4 Rarely.

Reviewing assessment, recording and reporting: identifying priorities for action

This summary of all the aspects of assessment recording and reporting arrangements (see Figure 7.10) will help you to pull together the various aspects of this area and to determine priorities for future development. A 1 to 4 ranking scale may help you to establish what these are.

The next chapter will consider the next step after monitoring – setting objectives for improvement.

Questions	Comments
Do teachers tell you about the progress you are making in your work?	
Is the marking of your work helpful?	
Do you understand the marking?	
How often do you read the teachers' comments?	
Do you mark your own work?	
Are you asked to think about how your work could be improved?	
Do you have targets for improving your work?	
Are end of year written reports useful to you?	
Do you keep any work as a permanent record? Who chooses it?	
Are results of tests discussed with you to help you to know how to improve?	
What improvements would you like to see most?	

© Bubb and Hoare 2001

Figure 7.9 A checklist to elicit children's views

Success criteria	Comments
The arrangements for assessment, recording and reporting meet statutory requirements	
Planning indicates assessment opportunities	
A range of assessment strategies (including observation) are evident in practice	
Marking practices comply with our policy and provide constructive dialogue with pupils	
Pupils understand our assessment practices and are involved in self-assessment	
Assessment and recording includes achievement in a broad range of contexts	
Arrangements for recording assessments are clear to all users and are followed	
Reports provide guidance on strengths and weaknesses	
Assessments are accurate and consistent	
Assessment data is used to set both individual and school targets	
Governors are involved in data analysis and the setting of targets for improvement	
Responsibilities for assessment, recording and reporting are clearly defined	
The policy for assessment, recording and reporting is up-to-date and clear to all those involved	
Arrangements for the assessment and review of pupils with special educational needs comply with the Code of Practice	
Assessment reflects the needs and approaches of the different subjects in the curriculum	
Responsibilities and arrangements for monitoring assessment practices are clear and effective	
Arrangements for reporting to parents are valued and supportive	
The policy is reviewed regularly to ensure its effectiveness	

Figure 7.10 Overall view of assessment in the school © Bubb and Hoare 2001

8 Setting and reviewing objectives

Setting objectives

Issues around setting objectives

The benefit of objective-setting as a way to manage steady improvement by children and adults is well recognised. Objectives provide a framework for teachers doing a complex job at a very fast pace. They encourage people to prioritise tasks and make best use of time and other resources, and teachers should feel a sense of achievement when objectives are met.

There are problems, however, with objectives. One teacher said,

> What is the point of setting objectives? I have to be able to do *everything* to be able to teach at all. If my planning, control, assessment, teaching strategies or whatever are not right everything falls apart.

She has a point. To be effective, all areas have to be met.

NQTs are not part of the statutory performance management because induction already contains termly assessment, setting objectives and reviewing progress. The induction tutor has a role similar to that of a team leader as the person in charge of an NQT's monitoring, support and assessment. The whole performance management process starts with the Career Entry Profile that identifies strengths and areas for development. At the end of the induction period NQTs will set objectives for performance management like all other staff.

Some teachers find that there is discussion about how they are doing but no specific objectives. The very act of writing them down causes people to consider whether they are the real priorities and gives teachers something to focus on. Occasionally objectives are set without the complete agreement of the teacher. This is usually counter-productive since the teacher is the one who has to be active in bringing about change. Some have said that the orally negotiated objectives change when written down.

A frequent problem with objectives is that they are not made specific enough, which can lead to failure. Bubb's research on NQTs (2000e) found that many objectives were too large so that they had to be repeated. For instance, one induction tutor wanted her NQT 'to teach the National Literacy and National Numeracy Strategies effectively'.

Objectives should be SMART: Specific, Measurable, Achievable, Realistic and Time-bound. This is of course also true of learning objectives in lesson plans or targets on Individual Education Plans (IEPs). Unfortunately this is easier said than done.

Individual Objectives and Action Plan

Teachers signature: Team leader's signature: Interview date: Review date:

Individual objectives (3–6)	Related school objectives	Actions (with date) to help meet objectives	Progress notes

© Bubb and Hoare 2001

Figure 8.1 Individual objectives and action plan

Consider an objective such as 'Improve control'. This may be too large, and could take a long time to achieve. It is better to be more specific about what needs most urgent attention, such as 'Improve control particularly after breaktimes, during independent activities and when tidying up'.

Always remember that objectives should be able to be met, while containing a degree of challenge. Look at those in Activity 8.1.

Activity 8.1
Setting objectives

These are the objectives set for an NQT at the end of their first term, to be met by the end of their second term. Looked at individually and as a whole what do you like and dislike about them? Are they all objectives or are any actions?

- Set clear aims at the beginning of every lesson and recap at the end to ensure that the children have made progress.
- Ensure that the lesson plan is referred to during the lesson and has clearly defined time limits to help inject pace and a sense of urgency into the lesson.
- Ensure that on records of work and lesson plans there is evidence that assessment informs planning.
- To look at realistic methods of differentiation.
- To incorporate greater use of ICT into lessons.
- To carry out observations of staff in other curriculum areas.

For performance management each teacher should have between three and six objectives for a year, at least one of which should be about pupil progress. This should be based on a realistic assessment of what pupils can be expected to achieve, based on what is already known about them. The other objectives should be about developing professional skills, and will give access to training. Objectives should also relate to job descriptions and the school development plan. They should be recorded in a format such as Figure 8.1.

Thinking of objectives that would last a year is difficult. Many of the objectives set lack challenge and will be hard to measure. Setting as annual objectives things one does already is futile. Look at the objectives in Activity 8.2. What do you think of them? Do they have enough challenge?

Some teachers have suffered from not having areas for development accurately diagnosed. It is very hard to decide what to work on when things are not going right because each problem has a huge knock on effect. As stated earlier, frequently objectives are not specific enough, which inevitably leads to failure when they are not met. Many objectives in the first term were too large and too long term so that they had to be repeated in the second term, but made more specific. The following is an example of one teacher's objectives:

First term:
To teach the National Literacy Strategy and National Numeracy Strategy effectively.
Second term:
To write focused learning objectives especially in the literacy hour and daily maths lesson.

Activity 8.2
Analysing objectives

These are the objectives of an experienced and successful teacher working in a nursery class:

Objective	Specific	Measurable	Achievable/ challenging	Time-bound
(a) That the majority of children are happy to leave parents and carers				
(b) To develop a good working relationship in the nursery team and begin to share planning				
(c) To ensure that the history curriculum is implemented throughout the school				

1. Say what you like and dislike about each objective, and what questions you would like to ask the teacher and team leader.

2. Say whether you think the objectives are specific, measurable, achievable/sufficiently challenging and time-bound.

To write specific group reading and writing targets.
To plan more manageable independent work in the literacy hour and daily maths lesson.

Imagine how the teacher felt not to be able to meet the first term's objective! She would have been able to make so much more progress had she been set the more detailed objectives in the first term. Always remember that objectives should be able to be met, while containing a degree of challenge.

Tips for objective setting

1. Think hard about the objective. Remember that your aim is to help the teacher improve the quality of learning of their pupils. Each of us has our own idiosyncratic emphases. So, someone's love of beautiful displays or hatred of worksheets, needs to be subsumed into looking at professionalism, planning and teaching. The biggest factor to remember is whether the weakness is having a detrimental effect on children's progress.

2. Think always of the objective setting dictum SMART. Objectives should be Specific, Measurable, Achievable, Realistic, Time-bound.
3. The objective needs to be very specific. This is of course also true of learning objectives in lesson plans or targets on an IEP. Consider objectives such as

   Improve subject knowledge in English
   Improve control
   Improve planning

   These are too large. It would be better to have a more specific aim.
4. Have between three and six objectives at a time. It is boosting if one objective is to develop a strength.
5. It is important that teachers feel ownership of the objectives. They should be jointly negotiated, with the teacher being proactive about identifying areas to develop, and how they can be achieved.
6. Objectives should be linked to the school development plan and have clear actions to help them be achieved. See Figure 8.1.

Writing an objective for pupil progress

The objective for pupil progress is very important, but hard to set. A useful tip is to link a teacher's objective for their class to the whole school target in the school development plan. The following modelling of the procedure for deciding on one comes from the DfEE website (www.dfee.gov.uk).

Consider the school's current plans and priorities
School priority identified to raise pupil's attainment in maths. (School Development/ Improvement Plan)
Consider the desired outcome
To raise pupil's attainment in maths.
Apply the SMART objective criteria (see Figure 8.2)
Final decision
   We suggest the following objective would be agreed:
   To manage the teaching and learning of maths in Key Stage 1 generally, and in particular Class B, to ensure maths scores increase by 2 per cent by July 2002.

The process of setting an objective for professional development and devising an action plan

When a teacher has a problem, it is essential that it is reflected upon and diagnosed accurately (Atton 2000) in order to draw up the most useful objectives and plan of action. I shall model how you could go about this using the example of a Year 2 teacher, Jenny, who needed a high level of support particularly with control.

1. The first thing to do when you have identified a problem is to brainstorm its features and results. For instance, Jenny's control problems include the following:
   – she lacks presence;
   – her voice is thin and becomes screechy when raised;

105

Analyse objective: To manage the teaching and learning of maths in Key Stage 1 generally, and in particular Class B, to ensure maths scores increase by 2 per cent by July 2002

Criteria	Questions	Answers
Specific Clear (Range) Concise	Is it a particular phase, year group, group or set of pupils? Which pupils – gender/ethnicity/ability/ special needs? Which subject? Any other relevant factors – level of exclusions?	Key Stage I Class B Maths
Measurable Able to be monitored Evidence-based Outcome measures	What evidence of attainment is there? Comparative data – other schools/ nationally? How should rise in attainment be measured – what evidence/data will it be based on? % SATS results increase/ teacher assessment?	% increase in SATS results at Key Stage 1
Achievable Challenging Realistic Resourced	What can be achieved? Level of challenge – low/medium/high? What are the current strengths/ weaknesses – what can we build on and what new things need to be done? Have we got resources and if not what needs to be done?	Level of challenge judged against level of improvement necessary and resources available
Relevant Impact Context Job Description (Accountability)	Will the objective achieve maximum impact? Assess objective for high/medium/low impact. Is the subject of the objective appropriate as a key priority for improvement? Can/how will the head address the objective? Within Job Description – is the objective appropriate to the role of the head? Is the objective relevant to the current school context now and within the estimated time of objective?	Yes – high impact
Time Related Milestones Review date	What will be the signs/evidence of progress made and performance indicators?	Interim pupil test results, teacher assessment and predictions with termly review dates

Figure 8.2 Apply the SMART criteria to an objective
(www.dfee.gov.uk/teachingreforms/rewards/perfmanage/govsobjectives)

– sometimes she comes down hard on the children and at other times she lets them get away with things;

– she takes a long time to get attention;

– she runs out of time so plenaries are missed, class is late to assembly, etc.;

– children call out;

– children are too noisy;

– a small group of children is behaving badly; and

– even the usually well-behaved children are being naughty.

Look at your list. Does it seem a fair picture? It is easy to be too hard or too generous.

2. List some positive features of the teacher, ideally relating to behaviour management. For instance, Jenny:

   – really likes and cares for the children;

   – speaks to them with respect;

   – plans interesting work for them;

   – is very effective when working with individuals or small groups;

   – has better control in the early part of the day; and

   – works hard.

3. With the teacher, think of when things go well and badly, as in Figure 8.3.

4. Discuss with the teacher why things go well using a format such as Figure 8.4. Reflection on successes is very powerful.

5. The process of analysing strengths is very boosting and this positive thinking can now be used to reflect on problem parts of the day. Figure 8.5 shows a format that could be used to analyse in fine detail when things go badly. In your discussion, try to tease out the reasons for deterioration in control. Help the teacher think of actions to remedy situations – they can be surprisingly easy!

6. Try now to encourage the teacher to think more generally about behaviour management. What aspects are the most urgent and achievable? Select up to three aspects. Any more than three things to work on at a time becomes very difficult.

   An action plan (see Figure 8.6) needs to be drawn up to help the teacher meet the objective. Thinking about the steps towards achieving an objective – the success criteria – will be essential. Then you can think of activities for the action plan. It should include:

   • the agreed objectives;

   • the actions to be taken to achieve them, and by whom;

   • the success criteria which will enable judgements to be made about the extent to which each objective has been met;

   • the resources, if any, that will be needed;

   • target dates for their achievement;

   • dates when progress will next be reviewed.

Some people find the format (see Figure 8.7 for a blank version) useful for unpacking one objective, or you could use the DfEE record suggested in the model performance management policy (DfEE 2000e). Look at Activity 8.3 to think about what would be useful activities for specific objectives for a nursery teacher.

Activity 8.3
Action Plans
These are the objectives of an experienced and successful teacher working in a nursery class. Write some suggestions for activities that could be included in an action plan.

Objective	Activities in an action plan
a) That 60 per cent of children will be able to achieve the early learning goals in maths by the time they leave the nursery.	
b) To develop a good working relationship in the nursery team and share planning.	
c) To ensure that the history curriculum is implemented throughout the school.	

When things go well	When things go badly
At the start of the morning	Often after lunchtime and playtimes End of the morning
At story-time	Tidying-up time
When I'm well prepared	Home time
When I've got a helper	When I'm on my own with the class
Literacy hour whole-class sessions	Literacy hour activities

Figure 8.3 Identifying when things go well and badly

When things go well	Why?
At the start of the morning	Children and teacher are fresh. Children and teacher know exactly what to do. Teacher greets children well. Good atmosphere. Grudges are forgotten
At story-time	Teacher reads stories brilliantly, captivating children – they can't wait for the next episode.
When I'm well prepared	Teacher feels confident when everything is well planned and resourced.
When I've got a helper	An extra person can focus on one table and keep an eye on another. Teacher has a good relationship with her, gives her plans and feels relaxed with her in the room.
Literacy hour whole-class sessions	Teacher prepares these well, thinking carefully about use of big books, etc. Questioning and use of talk partners works well to involve all pupils.

© Bubb and Hoare 2001

Figure 8.4 Analysing why things go well

When things go badly	Why?	Action
Often after lunchtime and playtimes	Arguments outside the classroom spill into teaching time. Teacher gets hassled trying to listen to everyone's point of view. This takes a long time, resulting in losing the rest of the class. Teacher loses teaching impetus.	
Tidying-up time	Most children do nothing except mess around, leaving the tidying to the same few girls. Noise level rises.	
Home time	Giving out reading folders, homework, letters, coats, etc., takes ages. Children get noisier. Teacher gets stressed about being late out to the playground.	
When I'm on my own with the class	The teacher is more inclined to panic when things go wrong when on her own.	
Literacy hour activities	Hard to find useful activities that can be done independently. Some children finish too early but most barely start. Noise level rises. Children wander around distracting teacher from focus group.	

© Bubb and Hoare 2001

Figure 8.5 Analysing why things go badly

Name: Jenny	Date: 1 November	Date objective to be met by: 13 December		
Objective: To improve control, particularly after playtimes, in independent literacy activities, at tidying-up time, and home time.				
Success criteria	**Actions**		**When**	**Progress**
Gets attention more quickly	Brainstorm attention-getting devices. Use triangle, etc., to get attention.			
Rarely shouts	Voice management course. Project the voice. Don't talk over children.			
Plans for behaviour management	Glean ideas from other teachers through discussion and observation. Watch videos on behaviour management strategies. Write notes for behaviour management on plans.			
Successful procedures for sorting out disputes after playtimes	Glean ideas from other teachers. Ask playground supervisors to note serious incidents. Children to post messages in incident box.			
Successful procedures for tidying	Discuss what other teachers do. Start tidying earlier and time it with reward for beating record. Sanctions for the lazy.			
Successful procedures for home time	Discuss ideas with other teachers. Monitors to organise things to take home. Start home time procedures earlier and time them (with rewards?)			
Children succeed in independent literacy activities	Ideas from literacy coordinator and adviser. Change seating for groups. Differentiate work. Discuss with additional adults.			
Review				

Figure 8.6 An action plan to meet an objective – an example

© Bubb and Hoare 2001

Name:	Date:	Date objective to be met by:		
Objective:				

Success criteria	Actions	When	Progress
Review			

© Bubb and Hoare 2001

Figure 8.7 An action plan to meet an objective – blank

Attending courses for professional development

An important decision that needs to be made is whether the teacher should go on courses. These are often run by local education authorities, higher education institutions and educational consultants. A major advantage of joining such a programme is that teachers gain a great deal from talking to each other. Enrolment on an externally organised programme also eases the burden on schools to provide training.

Advantages and disadvantages of attending courses

Advantages of going on a course	Disadvantages of going on a course
1. The teacher will meet many others from different schools and training institutions.	Teachers may become dissatisfied with their school when they hear about others.
2. The course should meet general needs well, easing the burden on schools.	The school can meet individual needs in their specific context.
3. Economy of scale should mean value for money.	With a limited budget the money might be better spent.
4. Teachers will learn from the practice of other schools and teachers.	It may not be feasible for several teachers from the same school to be out at the same time.
5. There will be time to reflect out of the school.	The time taken travelling to the courses may not be practical.
6. The course will cover subjects and topics that the school may not have the time or expertise to deliver.	The school may have staff with the time and expertise to run sessions that are focused on the teacher's individual context.
7. Many have tasks to do after sessions that encourage reflection and develop practice.	
8. Some courses are accredited so that teachers can move towards getting an Advanced Diploma or MA.	

© Bubb and Hoare 2001

The choice of course is also a matter for consideration. Quality and value for money are all important. There are the obvious benefits from attending the LEA programme: the teacher will be familiar with local advisers and initiatives and meet teachers from similar schools. Programmes run by higher education institutions or other LEAs may, however, be at a more convenient time and location.

It is essential that teachers use courses to become more effective. A record such as Figure 8.8 which demonstrates the effectiveness might be useful.

Date, time, venue	Subject	Things learnt that have influenced classroom practice

Figure 8.8 Record of training (in and out of school)

The Kirkpatrick model for training evaluation

In the 1950s Donald Kirkpatrick was a professor of marketing at the University of Wisconsin. He was responsible for developing and leading a project (Kirkpatrick 1959) to assess quality systems. His research revolved around three questions:

Why evaluate?
What to evaluate?
Who to evaluate for?

These questions have remained at the root of all training and attempts to improve systems through quality assurance. They are generally applied only in the business framework, although they have been raised before in many different professions. Before Kirkpatrick's work, no one had put forward a framework for consistent and constructive analysis. Kirkpatrick developed a four step framework, which was first published in 1959 in the *Journal of the American Society of Training Directors*.

There have been many variations on the model, but the Kirkpatrick model remains the benchmark against which most business training programmes are evaluated. This is primarily because of the simplicity of the model, how it relates to the trainee and the workplace and the way in which it can readily be applied to almost every type of work situation and learning process.

The Kirkpatrick model explores the relationship between training and the workplace at four levels:

- Reactions
- Learning
- Behaviour
- Results.

These are measured at suitable points during the training process. The first three are essentially trainee based, while the fourth changes emphasis and centres on the effectiveness of the training for the organisation.

Level One: Reactions

By evaluating reactions, you find out if participants enjoyed the training, if the training environment was suitable and comfortable and if the trainers were capable and credible. In short, you are trying to learn what participants think and feel about the training.

Level Two: Learning

By evaluating learning, you determine the extent to which trainees have done the following three things as a result of their training: changed their attitudes, improved their knowledge or increased their skills.

Level Three: Behaviour

By evaluating behaviour, you determine if the trainees are using or transferring their newly learned knowledge, skills and behaviours back on the job. In other words, what behaviour changed because people took part in a training session?

Level Four: Results

By evaluating results, you determine if the training has affected school results or contributed to the achievement of an objective. This final evaluation which considers both personal evaluation and company benefit makes the Kirkpatrick model so suitable for so many types of training.

The value of the Kirkpatrick approach is that it creates a process for consistent and structured learning evaluation. This is important in relation to developing and promoting the skills central to performance management. For multi-site business operations this ensures consistency of assessment and employee/corporation progress. There is a direct parallel between this business model and the situation of a local education authority overseeing a range of schools. It is also important where an organisation is aiming for external recognition of the quality of its training, such as the UK Investors in People programme. Evaluating results is one of the most critical and difficult elements of this programme. Following the Kirkpatrick model in a controlled learning environment makes meeting the requirements of this type of requirement relatively straightforward.

Reviewing objectives

Everyone should be encouraged to log, albeit briefly, their progress in meeting the performance management objectives during the year. The team leader should be aware of teachers' progress through appropriate monitoring and take any supportive action needeed. However, there should be a formal annual performance management review meeting at the end of year. Sending a letter (such as the one below) to the teacher will aid this feeling of greater formality.

Dear

Performance Management Review Meeting

Your performance management review will be held on

The purpose of the meeting is for us to celebrate your strengths, evaluate progress in meeting the objectives for the last year and discuss ones for the next twelve months. Please bring your professional portfolio and your pupil assessment folder.

Objectives should help you develop professionaly, raise your pupils' achievement and contribute to the whole school's improvement. According to our performance management policy at least one objective should be for your professional development and one for pupil progress. There can be a minimum of three and a maximum of six. It would be useful to come to the interview with some ideas of what areas you would like to develop. These should be informed by the school development plan, a copy of which is enclosed.

I look forward to meeting with you.

Yours sincerely

Team Leader

The performance management review cycle ends with an annual review at which the team leader discusses a teacher's performance in a structured way, recognising achievements and identifying developmental needs. The objectives should be used as a focus to make a professional judgement about overall effectiveness. In most schools the formal review meeting will be held towards the end of the school year when pupils' test results, or whatever measure of progress there is in place, have been analysed. The meeting should be motivating, participative and supportive to improve committment and responsibility. At the meeting you should cover the following:

- discuss progress in meeting the objectives;
- celebrate strengths and successes;
- analyse the reasons for not meeting any objectives;
- discuss and set new ones that are clear, challenging and realistic.

Ask the teacher to do a self-evaluation. This reflection will be very useful for both of you. Comparing notes will give you an up-to-date and often very detailed picture. Be aware, however, that the majority of teachers have very high expectations of themselves and will consider some things weaknesses that are perfectly fine.

Evidence to inform the review meeting

It is essential that the assessment meeting is based on hard evidence. This may take various forms, such as:

- records of observations and the follow-up discussions;
- records from meetings;
- self-assessment by the teacher;
- analysis of pupils' work and assessment records;
- monitored samples of the teacher's planning and lesson evaluations;
- information about the teacher's wider professional effectiveness, particularly for areas of responsibility such as subject leadership.

Performance review statements

The team leader needs to write a performance review statement and give a copy to the teacher within ten days of the meeting. The teacher should have ten days in which to add written comments. Then the completed, review statement is passed to the head teacher. At the time of writing, there was no detailed guidance as to what a performance review statement should contain.

How to go about writing the statement
1. Focus on criteria that need to be commented on, and the progress in meeting each objective.
2. Write the statement *about*, not *to* the teacher. Adopt a formal style.
3. Write concisely, being careful to make the wording clear and professional. It should be brief (no more than one page of A4) and word-processed so that amendments can be made easily.
4. Decide what you think are the main issues. If there are weaknesses, diagnose the root of the problem and focus on that.

5. Be positive – we can cope with criticism if our good points celebrated. Be effusive in praising strengths, but make sure your message is clear, especially where there are areas of weakness.
6. Refer briefly to the evidence for your judgements, particularly in terms of pupil progress. Ideally, there will be no surprises if points have been raised throughout the year.
7. Write the new objectives that you agreed with the teacher. Apply the SMART criteria.
8. Check it for errors – spelling mistakes are so embarrassing! Give it to the teacher for comment for up to ten days. When both of you are happy with the statement send a copy to the head teacher.

The last chapter focuses on crossing the threshold, with ideas on how to complete the threshold application form and keeping a professional portfolio.

9 Preparing to cross the threshold

Threshold assessment

The threshold is the next assessable point after induction. When you have reached salary spine point 9 you can apply to 'cross the threshold', which increases your salary by £2,000. If you get the typical one annual increment, you will reach it after seven years or so. The length of time depends on what point you start on – whether you are a good honours graduate and if you have other relevant experience. If you are on the Fast-track you will be expected to reach spine point 9 in five years.

There are eight threshold standards. They cover five areas, all of which relate directly or indirectly to classroom teaching: knowledge and understanding; teaching and assessment; pupil progress; wider professional effectiveness; and professional characteristics. There are three standards in the teaching and assessment area. There are two standards under wider professional effectiveness.

Knowledge and Understanding: Teachers should demonstrate that they have a thorough and up-to-date knowledge of the teaching of their subject(s) and take account of wider curriculum developments, which are relevant to their work.

Teaching and Assessment: Teachers should demonstrate that they consistently and effectively:

- plan lessons and sequences of lessons to meet pupils' individual learning needs
- use a range of appropriate strategies for teaching and classroom management
- use information about prior learning to set well-grounded expectations for pupils and monitor progress to give clear and constructive feedback.

Pupil Progress: Teachers should demonstrate that, as a result of their teaching, their pupils achieve well relative to the pupils' prior attainment, making progress as good or better than similar pupils nationally. This should be shown in marks or grades in any relevant national tests or examinations, or school based assessments for pupils where national tests and examinations are not taken.

Wider Professional Effectiveness: Teachers should demonstrate that they:

- take responsibility for their professional development and use the outcomes to improve their teaching and pupils' learning
- make an active contribution to the policies and aspirations of the school.

Professional Characteristics: Teachers should demonstrate that they are effective professionals who challenge and support all pupils to do their best through:

inspiring trust and confidence
building team commitment
engaging and motivating pupils
analytic thinking
positive action to improve the quality of pupils' learning.

(DfEE 2000g)

The teacher is responsible for applying for assessment. This involves summarising evidence – in the form of concrete examples from the applicant's day-to-day work – to show that he or she has worked at broadly the standards indicated over the last two to three years. The assessment is made by the head teacher who has a legal and professional responsibility for evaluating the standards of teaching and learning in the school and ensuring that proper standards of professional performance are established and maintained. The accredited external assessors will work with head teachers to verify, on a sampling basis, that the threshold standards are being applied fairly and consistently both within the school and across schools.

Completing the threshold application form

Filling in forms is something that most people hate. In 2000, the first cohort of eligible people found the threshold form very difficult to complete because everything was new. Keeping the threshold standards in mind during the first years of your career will make this process easier, as will keeping a professional portfolio (Figure 9.1). Figure 9.2 has some prompts to help you complete each section of the form.

The professional portfolio

Contents

1. CV – career history
   References
   Job description
   Qualifications
2. Courses
   List of courses and INSET attended
   Certificates from courses attended
   Reflection on how you implemented ideas gained from the courses
3. Other professional development
   Articles read
   Websites visited
4. Monitoring of your teaching
   Feedback on your planning
   Feedback on your teaching from lesson observations
   Feedback on your assessments
   OFSTED grades
5. Subject leader role
   Development plan and dated achievements
   Staff meetings and INSET
   OFSTED and LEA reports on your subject
6. Pupil progress
   Data showing progress
   SEN
7. Objectives
   Action plans
   Reviews of progress

© Bubb and Hoare 2001

Figure 9.1 The professional portfolio – contents

Threshold: Prompts for Teachers

Deciding to apply . . .

1. Do I want to apply? Am I eligible?

Planning an application . . .

2. Read standards, application form and guidance notes. Watch the school's threshold video. Think about how I demonstrate the standards in my day-to-day teaching. What information is collected centrally in my school on which I can draw?

3. What evidence to present? Requirement is to summarise evidence under each heading – in terms of practical examples from day-to-day work and cite sources. Evidence needs to cover all eight standards – they all need to be met.

4. **Important:** I need a brief description of the way I teach. Based on concrete examples, not assertions. I should know how to access key pieces of supporting evidence but there is no need to collect them or attach them.

5. Is the application short and factual and does it give a good feel for how I teach? Bullet points are preferable to extended prose. Have all the standards been covered? Remember to keep a photocopy.

   For example, don't say: 'I made a report to the governing body about . . .' Do say: 'My report to the governing body showed good progress in . . .'

Evidence about Knowledge and Understanding . . .

6. Does my teaching reflect accepted good practice in my subject(s)? How do I keep up-to-date on content? Through subject associations?

7. Do I have a good knowledge of my subject(s) or specialism(s)? How have I kept up-to-date? If I am teaching outside my specialism how did I adapt/retrain?

8. Have I extended my knowledge to take account of wider curriculum changes (e.g. Early Learning Goals for KS1 teacher; KS2 changes for a KS3 teacher) If so, how?

9. Do I need to take account of national literacy, numeracy and ICT strategies? How have I done so? What have I done to develop my ability to use ICT in my teaching? NB: ICT to be assessed in the context of training and the access you have to equipment and software.

   Potential sources of evidence: schemes of work and policies; lesson plans; OFSTED grades and feedback from observation; presentations given; use of ICT to extend pupil resources/e-mail/Internet; active membership of subject associations/liaison groups/professional association committees; qualifications obtained; command of National Curriculum.

Evidence about Teaching and Assessment . . .

10. The three standards in this area are about showing consistent and effective performance in planning, in teaching and classroom management and in the use of assessment. They are about your teaching, not your pupils' learning. What examples can I cite? Classroom observation? OFSTED assessment?

    For example, don't say, 'I make sure my teaching is appropriate to each child's needs. Do say: 'Feedback from observation/OFSTED praised the way . . . My coursework/lesson planner, show how . . . Homework is regularly marked and available to show how . . .'.

11. How can I show that I consistently and effectively plan lessons and sequences of lessons to meet pupils' individual learning needs?

    How does my lesson planning reflect the learning needs of the children I teach?
    Do I communicate learning objectives to pupils?
    Do I make use of homework effectively?

Figure 9.2 Threshold Prompts (DfEE 2000g)

Potential sources of evidence: termly/weekly lesson plans; session notes/evaluation; up-to-date planners; lesson objectives communicated to pupils; homework regularly set and marked; log of calls to parents/discussions with parents; Individual Educational Plans; discussions with pupils and colleagues.

12. Do I consistently and effectively use a range of appropriate teaching and learning strategies and classroom management techniques? What examples should I have of particular strategies I use to promote pupils' progress?

Do I vary teaching and learning strategies and classroom management techniques to motivate different pupils?

Do I give targeted support for pupils with particular learning needs, and keep good levels of behaviour and discipline?

Do I manage the time and people resources available to me?

Potential sources of evidence: feedback from lesson observations or other visits; use of classroom space; examples of differentiated worksheets or lesson plans; support sought for individual pupils from SENCO, etc.; involvement of classroom assistant or learning support assistant; use of technicians; use of other school resources.

13. How can I show I use information about prior attainment to set well-grounded expectations for pupils and monitor progress to give clear and constructive feedback?

Do I use information about prior attainment to set challenging but realistic targets for pupils?

Do I use assessment as part of my everyday work to monitor progress and adapt my approach if necessary?

Do I use this information to give clear and positive feedback?

Potential sources of evidence: books marked in line with school policy; assessments and analysis of pupils' work; monitoring by curriculum leaders and others in line with school assessment policy; reports to parents and subject/year leaders.

Evidence about Pupil Progress . . .

14. What records do I have about the progress my pupils have made? What national tests or assessments can I use which show prior attainment and progress achieved? If none of these are relevant, what school based assessments can I show? Is there relevant information in my school's PANDA about how our progress compares with that in schools in similar contexts?

15. Which groups of pupils are representative of the range of my work? Need to choose two or three classes or subjects. For each of them give:

Brief context to explain the information? Which sets taught (if appropriate)? Any particular factors to be taken into account in reviewing it?

Baseline information about prior attainment.

How progress is monitored in line with school assessment policy.

What progress is expected, and how does this relate to national levels of achievement in my subject(s) or specialism(s)?

Progress made.

Evaluation of progress.

Evidence about Wider Professional Effectiveness . . .

16. What have I personally done to pursue my own professional development (in the broadest sense)? What activities inside or outside schools (not just courses) have I made use of to improve my teaching? What has been the effect?

17. How do I contribute through my teaching and other work to the school development plan, to the implementation of school policies and to the wider aspirations and values of the school? (Voluntary activities are not essential to answer this although they can be cited if relevant.)

Figure 9.2 *cont.*

Potential sources of evidence: types of professional development undertaken; distance learning/own-time study; provision of information to colleagues; mentoring; involvement in formulation and promotion of school policies; personal research; visits to other departments and schools and comparing approaches; parental partnerships; involvement in school development plan.

Evidence about Professional Characteristics . . .

18. What is it that makes me a good teacher? What has not already been covered in my evidence?

19. How do I: Inspire trust and confidence? Build team commitment? Engage and motivate pupils? Think analytically and creatively about my work? Take positive steps to improve the quality of pupils' learning?

20. What examples can I cite, e.g. about the way I try to generate an atmosphere where pupils are not afraid to express themselves or make mistakes? Provide help and support for colleagues? Value ideas and input? Know what will appeal to pupils and persuade them to perform? How do I plan my lesson on the basis of my analysis of pupil performance? Give individualised feedback? Provide stimulating and relevant opportunities for pupils to learn?

Potential sources of evidence: pastoral and extracurricular activities; lesson observation; planning file; rewards system for pupils; feedback from pupils/parents/colleagues; team activities; diagnostic assessments; staff minutes/annual reviews; representing school at meetings, conferences.

Figure 9.2 *cont.*

Appendix:
Standards for the award of Qualified Teacher Status (DfEE Circular 4/98)

A. KNOWLEDGE AND UNDERSTANDING

1. Secondary

Those to be awarded QTS must, when assessed, demonstrate that they:

a. have a secure knowledge and understanding of the concepts and skills in their specialist subject(s) at a standard equivalent to degree level to enable them to teach it (them) confidently and accurately at:

   i. KS3 for trainees on 7–14 courses;

   ii. KS3 and KS4 and, where relevant, post-16 for trainees on 11–16 or 18 courses; and

   iii. KS4 and post-16 for trainees on 14–19 courses;

b. **for English, mathematics or science specialists,** have a secure knowledge and understanding of the subject content specified in the relevant Initial Teacher Training National Curriculum[1];

c. have, for their specialist subject(s), where applicable, a detailed knowledge and understanding of the National Curriculum programmes of study, level descriptions or end of key stage descriptions for KS3 and, where applicable, National Curriculum programmes of study for KS4;

d. for Religious Education (RE) specialists, have a detailed knowledge of the Model Syllabuses for RE;

e. are familiar, for their specialist subject(s), with the relevant KS4 and post-16 examination syllabuses and courses, including vocational courses;

f. understand, for their specialist subject(s), the framework of 14–19 qualifications and the routes of progression through it[2];

g. understand, for their specialist subject(s), progression from the KS2 programmes of study[3];

h. know and can teach the key skills required for current qualifications relevant to their specialist subject(s), for pupils aged 14–19, and understand the contribution that their specialist subject(s) make(s) to the development of the key skills[2];

i. cope securely with subject-related questions which pupils raise;

---

1 This does not apply until September 1999.
2 This does not apply to trainees on 7–14 courses.
3 This does not apply to trainees on 14–19 courses.

j. are aware of, and know how to access, recent inspection evidence and classroom-relevant research evidence on teaching secondary pupils in their specialist subject(s), and know how to use this to inform and improve their teaching;

k. know, for their specialist subject(s), pupils' most common misconceptions and mistakes;

l. understand how pupils' learning in the subject is affected by their physical, intellectual, emotional and social development;

m. have, for their specialist subject(s), a secure knowledge and understanding of the content specified in the ITT National Curriculum for Information and Communications Technology in subject teaching;

n. are familiar with subject-specific health and safety requirements, where relevant, and plan lessons to avoid potential hazards.

2. Primary

For all courses those to be awarded QTS must, when assessed, demonstrate that they:

a. understand the purposes, scope, structure and balance of the National Curriculum Orders as a whole and, within them, the place and scope of the primary phase, the key stages, the primary core and foundation subjects and RE;

b. are aware of the breadth of content covered by the pupils' National Curriculum across the primary core and foundation subjects and RE;

c. understand how pupils' learning is affected by their physical, intellectual, emotional and social development.

d. for each core and specialist subject[4] covered in their training:

    i.   have, where applicable, a detailed knowledge and understanding of the relevant National Curriculum programmes of study and level descriptions or end of key stage descriptions across the primary age range;

    ii.   for RE specialists, have a detailed knowledge of the Model Syllabuses for RE;

    iii.   cope securely with subject-related questions which pupils raise;

    iv.   understand the progression from SCAA's *Desirable Outcomes for Children's Learning on Entering Compulsory Education* to KS1, the progression from KS1 to KS2, and from KS2 to KS3;

    v.   are aware of, and know how to access, recent inspection evidence and classroom relevant research evidence on teaching primary pupils in the subject, and know how to use this to inform and improve their teaching;

    vi.   know pupils' most common misconceptions and mistakes in the subject;

    vii.   have a secure knowledge and understanding of the content specified in the ITT National Curriculum for Information and Communications Technology in subject teaching;

    viii.   are familiar with subject-specific health and safety requirements, where relevant, and plan lessons to avoid potential hazards;

---

4 A specialist subject may be one of the core subjects.

e. for English, mathematics and science, have a secure knowledge and understanding of the subject content specified in the ITT National Curricula for primary English, mathematics and science[5];

f. for any specialist subject(s), have a secure knowledge of the subject to at least a standard approximating to GCE Advanced level in those aspects of the subject taught at KS1 and KS2;

g. for any non-core, non-specialist subject covered in their training, have a secure knowledge to a standard equivalent to at least level 7 of the pupils' National Curriculum. For RE, the required standard for non-specialist training is broadly equivalent to the end of key stage statements for Key Stage 4 in QCA's Model Syllabuses for RE[6].

3. Additional Standards relating to early years (nursery and reception) for trainees on 3–8 and 3–11 courses

Those to be awarded QTS must, when assessed, demonstrate that they:

a. have a detailed knowledge of SCAA's *Desirable Outcomes for Children's Learning on Entering Compulsory Education;*

b. have a knowledge of effective ways of working with parents and other carers;

c. have an understanding of the roles and responsibilities of other agencies with responsibility for the care of young children.

B. PLANNING, TEACHING AND CLASS MANAGEMENT

This section details the Standards which all those to be awarded QTS must demonstrate, when assessed, in each subject that they have been trained to teach. For primary non-core, non-specialist subjects, trainees being assessed for QTS must meet the required Standards but with the support, if necessary, of a teacher experienced in the subject concerned.

1. Primary English, mathematics and science

For all courses, those to be awarded QTS must, when assessed, demonstrate that they:

a. have a secure knowledge and understanding of, and know how and when to apply, the teaching and assessment methods specified in the ITT National Curricula for primary English, mathematics and science[5];

b. have a secure knowledge and understanding of, and know when to apply in relation to each subject, the teaching and assessment methods specified in the ITT National Curriculum for Information and Communications Technology in subject teaching.

---

5 For primary science this does not apply until September 1999.

6 Where providers offer more limited coverage of subjects than the required non-core, non-specialist subjects, **e.g. a few hours of taster training in a foundation subject, safety training in PE and/or design and technology,** the nature and extent of such training can be recorded on the newly qualified teacher's TTA Career Entry Profile.

2. Primary and secondary specialist subjects

For all courses, those to be awarded QTS must, when assessed, demonstrate that they have a secure knowledge and understanding of, and know how and when to apply, in relation to their specialist subject(s), the teaching and assessment methods specified in the ITT National Curriculum for Information and Communications Technology in subject teaching.

3. Secondary English, mathematics and science

To be awarded QTS specialists in secondary English, mathematics or science must, when assessed, demonstrate that they have a secure knowledge and understanding of, and know how and when to apply, the teaching and assessment methods specified in the relevant ITT National Curriculum[1].

4. Primary and secondary for all subjects

Planning

For all courses, those to be awarded QTS must, when assessed, demonstrate that they:

a. plan their teaching to achieve progression in pupils' learning through:

  i. identifying clear teaching objectives and content, appropriate to the subject matter and the pupils being taught, and specifying how these will be taught and assessed;

  ii. setting tasks for whole class, individual and group work, including homework, which challenge pupils and ensure high levels of pupil interest;

  iii. setting appropriate and demanding expectations for pupils' learning, motivation and presentation of work;

  iv. setting clear objectives for pupils' learning, building on prior attainment, and ensuring that pupils are aware of the substance and purpose of what they are asked to do;
  v. identifying pupils who:

  - have special educational needs, including specific learning difficulties;
  - are very able;
  - are not yet fluent in English;

  and knowing where to get help in order to give positive and targeted support;

b. provide clear structures for lessons, and for sequences of lessons, in the short, medium and longer term, which maintain pace, motivation and challenge for pupils;

c. make effective use of assessment information on pupils' attainment and progress in their teaching and in planning future lessons and sequences of lessons;

d. plan opportunities to contribute to pupils' personal, spiritual, moral, social and cultural development;

e. where applicable, ensure coverage of the relevant examination syllabuses and National Curriculum programmes of study.

Teaching and Class Management

For all courses, those to be awarded QTS must, when assessed, demonstrate that they:

f. ensure effective teaching of whole classes, and of groups and individuals within the whole class setting, so that teaching objectives are met, and best use is made of available teaching time;

g. monitor and intervene when teaching to ensure sound learning and discipline;

h. establish and maintain a purposeful working atmosphere;

i. set high expectations for pupils' behaviour, establishing and maintaining a good standard of discipline through well focused teaching and through positive and productive relationships;

j. establish a safe environment which supports learning and in which pupils feel secure and confident;

k. use teaching methods which sustain the momentum of pupils' work and keep all pupils engaged through:

   i.   stimulating intellectual curiosity, communicating enthusiasm for the subject being taught, fostering pupils' enthusiasm and maintaining pupils' motivation;

   ii. matching the approaches used to the subject matter and the pupils being taught;

   iii. structuring information well, including outlining content and aims, signalling transitions and summarising key points as the lesson progresses;

   iv. clear presentation of content around a set of key ideas, using appropriate subject-specific vocabulary and well chosen illustrations and examples;

   v.   clear instruction and demonstration, and accurate well-paced explanation;

   vi. effective questioning which matches the pace and direction of the lesson and ensures that pupils take part;

   vii. careful attention to pupils' errors and misconceptions, and helping to remedy them;

   viii. listening carefully to pupils, analysing their responses and responding constructively in order to take pupils' learning forward;

   ix. selecting and making good use of textbooks, ICT and other learning resources which enable teaching objectives to be met;

   x.   providing opportunities for pupils to consolidate their knowledge and maximising opportunities, both in the classroom and through setting well-focused homework, to reinforce and develop what has been learnt;

   xi. exploiting opportunities to improve pupils' basic skills in literacy, numeracy and ICT, and the individual and collaborative study skills needed for effective learning, including information retrieval from libraries, texts and other sources;

   xii. exploiting opportunities to contribute to the quality of pupils' wider educational development, including their personal, spiritual, moral, social and cultural development;

   xiii. setting high expectations for all pupils notwithstanding individual differences, including gender, and cultural and linguistic backgrounds;

xiv. providing opportunities to develop pupils' wider understanding by relating their learning to real and work-related examples;

l. are familiar with the Code of Practice on the identification and assessment of special educational needs and, as part of their responsibilities under the Code, implement and keep records on individual education plans (IEPs) for pupils at stage 2 of the Code and above;

m. ensure that pupils acquire and consolidate knowledge, skills and understanding in the subject;

n. evaluate their own teaching critically and use this to improve their effectiveness.

5. **Additional Standards relating to early years (nursery and reception) for trainees on 3–8 and 3–11 courses**

For all courses, those to be awarded QTS must, when assessed, demonstrate that they:

a. plan activities which take account of pupils' needs and their developing physical, intellectual, emotional and social abilities, and which engage their interest;

b. provide structured learning opportunities which advance pupils':

    i. personal and social development;

    ii. communication skills;

    iii. knowledge and understanding of the world;

    iv. physical development;

    v. creative development;

c. use teaching approaches and activities which develop pupils' language and provide the foundations for literacy;

d. use teaching approaches and activities which develop pupils' mathematical understanding and provide the foundations for numeracy;

e. encourage pupils to think and talk about their learning and to develop self-control and independence;

f. encourage pupils to concentrate and persevere in their learning for sustained periods, to listen attentively and to talk about their experiences in small and large groups;

g. use teaching approaches and activities which involve planned adult intervention, which offer opportunities for first-hand experience and co-operation, and which use play and talk as a vehicle for learning;

h. manage, with support from an experienced specialist teacher if necessary, the work of parents and other adults in the classroom to enhance learning opportunities for pupils.

C. MONITORING, ASSESSMENT, RECORDING, REPORTING AND ACCOUNTABILITY

This section details the Standards which all those to be awarded QTS must demonstrate, when assessed, in each subject that they have been trained to teach. For primary non-core, non-specialist subjects, trainees being assessed for QTS must meet the required Standards but with the support, if necessary, of a teacher experienced in the subject concerned.

For all courses, those to be awarded QTS must, when assessed, demonstrate that they:

a. assess how well learning objectives have been achieved and use this assessment to improve specific aspects of teaching;

b. mark and monitor pupils' assigned classwork and homework, providing constructive oral and written feedback, and setting targets for pupils' progress;

c. assess and record each pupil's progress systematically, including through focused obser-vation, questioning, testing and marking, and use these records to:

   i. check that pupils have understood and completed the work set;

   ii. monitor strengths and weaknesses and use the information gained as a basis for purposeful intervention in pupils' learning;

   iii. inform planning;

   iv. check that pupils continue to make demonstrable progress in their acquisition of the knowledge, skills and understanding of the subject;

d. are familiar with the statutory assessment and reporting requirements and know how to prepare and present informative reports to parents;

e. where applicable, understand the expected demands of pupils in relation to each relevant level description or end of key stage description, and, in addition, for those on 11–16 or 18 and 14–19 courses, the demands of the syllabuses and course requirements for GCSE, other KS4 courses, and, where applicable, post-16 courses;

f. where applicable, understand and know how to implement the assessment requirements of current qualifications for pupils aged 14–19;

g. recognise the level at which a pupil is achieving, and assess pupils consistently against attainment targets, where applicable, if necessary with guidance from an experienced teacher;

h. understand and know how national, local, comparative and school data, including National Curriculum test data, where applicable, can be used to set clear targets for pupils' achievement;

i. use different kinds of assessment appropriately for different purposes, including National Curriculum and other standardised tests, and baseline assessment where relevant.

D. OTHER PROFESSIONAL REQUIREMENTS

Primary and secondary

For all courses, those to be awarded QTS should, when assessed, demonstrate that they:

a. have a working knowledge and understanding of:

   i. teachers' professional duties as set out in the current School Teachers' Pay and Conditions document, issued under the School Teachers' Pay and Conditions Act 1991;

   ii. teachers' legal liabilities and responsibilities relating to:

- the Race Relations Act 1976;
- the Sex Discrimination Act 1975;
- Section 7 and Section 8 of the Health and Safety at Work etc. Act 1974;
- teachers' common law duty to ensure that pupils are healthy and safe on school premises and when leading activities off the school site, such as educational visits, school outings or field trips;
- what is reasonable for the purposes of safeguarding or promoting children's welfare (Section 3(5) of the Children Act 1989);
- the role of the education service in protecting children from abuse (currently set out in DfEE Circular 10/95 and the Home Office, Department of Health, DfEE and Welsh Office Guidance *Working Together: A guide to arrangements for inter-agency co-operation for the protection of children from abuse 1991*);
- appropriate physical contact with pupils (currently set out in DfEE Circular 10/95);
- appropriate physical restraint of pupils (Section 4 of the Education Act 1997 and DfEE Circular 9/94);
- detention of pupils on disciplinary grounds (Section 5 of the Education Act 1997);

b. have established, during work in schools, effective working relationships with professional colleagues including, where applicable, associate staff;

c. set a good example to the pupils they teach, through their presentation and their personal and professional conduct;

d. are committed to ensuring that every pupil is given the opportunity to achieve their potential and meet the high expectations set for them;

e. understand the need to take responsibility for their own professional development and to keep up-to-date with research and developments in pedagogy and in the subjects they teach;

f. understand their professional responsibilities in relation to school policies and practices, including those concerned with pastoral and personal safety matters, including bullying;

g. recognise that learning takes place inside and outside the school context, and understand the need to liaise effectively with parents and other carers and with agencies with responsibility for pupils' education and welfare;

h. are aware of the role and purpose of school governing bodies.

Bibliography

ACAS (1990) *Appraisal Related Pay*. Advisory Booklet No. 11. London: ACAS.

Atton, T. (2000) 'When staff fail: understanding and managing poor performance', *Professional Development Today* **3**(2).

Beresford, J. (1999) *Collecting Information for School Improvement. Model questionnaires and research instruments*. London: David Fulton Publishers.

Birmingham LEA (2000) *Signposts Baseline Assessment*, Rvd edn. Birmingham: Birmingham LEA.

Brighouse, T. and Moon, B. (1995) *School Inspection*. London: Pitman Publishing.

Bubb, S. (2000a) *The Effective Induction of Newly Qualified Primary Teachers: An induction tutor's handbook*. London: David Fulton Publishers.

Bubb, S. (2000b) 'Caution: danger ahead – newly qualified teachers' induction standards', *Times Educational Supplement*, 14 January.

Bubb, S. (2000c) 'The Spying Game – observing teachers', *Times Educational Supplement*, 5 May.

Bubb, S. (2000d) 'More than a mentor – the induction tutor's role', *Times Educational Supplement*, 7 July.

Bubb, S. (2000e) 'Statutory induction – a fair deal for all?', *Institute of Education Viewpoint* 12.

Bubb, S. (2001) *A Newly Qualified Teacher's Manual*. London: David Fulton Publishers.

Bubb, S. and Burrell, A. (2000) 'Teacher feedback in the reception class: associations with children's positive adjustment to school', *Education 3–13* **28**(3), 58–64.

Bullough, R. V. (1989) *First-Year Teacher – a case study*. New York: Teachers' College Press.

Clarke, S. (1998) *Targetting Assessment in the Primary Classroom*. London: Hodder and Stoughton.

DfEE (1998a) *Supporting the Target Setting Process: Guidance for effective target setting for pupils with special educational needs*. London: QCA.

DfEE (1998b) *Teaching: High Status, High Standards*. Circular 4/98. London: DfEE.

DfEE (1998c) *Reducing the Bureaucratic Burden on Teachers*. Circular 02/98. London: DfEE.

DfEE (1998d) *Teachers Meeting the Challenge of Change*. Green Paper. London: DfEE.

DfEE (1999a) *The Induction Period for Newly Qualified Teachers*. Circular 5/99. London: DfEE.

DfEE (1999b) *Getting the Most from your Data*. London: DfEE AUTLEAF 3-4.

DfEE (1999c) *Performance Management*. London: DfEE.

DfEE (2000a) *Curriculum Guidance for the Foundation Stage*. London: QCA.

DfEE (2000b) *Baseline Assessment for the Foundation Stage – a consultation*. London: QCA.

DfEE (2000c) *Recognising Progress – Getting the most from your data*. DfEE 0253/2000.

DfEE (2000d) *School Teachers' Pay and Conditions of Employment*. London: DfEE.

DfEE (2000e) *Performance Management Model Policy*. London: DfEE.

DfEE (2000f) *Performance Managment: Toolkit for PMCs*. London: DfEE.

DfEE (2000g) *Threshold Assessment*. London: DfEE.

Draper, I. (2000) 'Beyond appraisal', *Managing Schools Today* **10**(2).

Earley, P. and Kinder, K. (1994) *Initiation Rights – Effective Induction Practices for New Teachers*. Slough: NFER.

Edgington, M. (1998) *The Nursery Teacher in Action*. PCP Publishing.

Eraut, M. (1994) *Developing Professional Knowledge and Competence*. London: Falmer Press.

Ghaye, A. and Ghaye, K. (1998) *Teaching and Learning through Critical Reflective Practice*. London: David Fulton Publishers.

Gipps, C. and Clarke, S. (1998) *Monitoring Consistency in Teacher Assessment and the Impact of SCAA's Guidance Materials at Key Stages 1, 2, and 3*. London: QCA.

Gipps, C. *et al.* (1996) 'Models of teacher assessment among primary school teachers in England', *The Curriculum Journal* **7**(2), 167–83.

Gipps, C. *et al.* (1998) 'The role of the teacher in National Assessment in England', AERA Conference, San Diego 1998.

Goldstein, H. *et al.* (2000) *The Use of Value Added Information in Judging School Performance*. London: Institute of Education.

Hagger, H. and McIntyre, D. (1994) 'Monitoring in secondary schools.' *Reading 8: Learning Through Analysing Practice*. Milton Keynes: Open University.

Hagger, H. *et al.* (1993) *The School Mentor Handbook*. London: Kogan Page.

Hay McBer (2000) http://www.dfee.gov.uk/teachingreforms/leadership/mcber/

Hustler, D. and McIntyre, D. (eds) (1996) *Developing Competent Teachers*. London: David Fulton Publishers.

Ironside, M. and Siefert, R. (1995) *Industrial Relations in Schools*. London: Routledge.

Islington Education (1999) *Early Years Curriculum Guidelines for Babies to Five-Year-Olds*. London: Islington Council Education Services.

Kendall, L. *et al.* (2000) *Investors in People in Schools*. London: NFER/DfEE.

Kirkpatrick, D. (1959) 'The Kirkpatrick model for training evaluation', *The Journal of the American Society of Training Directors* **III**, August.

Lindsay, G. *et al.* (July 2000) *Evaluation of accredited baseline assessment schemes 1999/2000*. CEDAR, University of Warwick

Malderez, A. and Bodoczky, C. (1999) *Mentor Courses – a resource book for trainers*. Cambridge: Cambridge University Press.

Maynard, T. and Furlong, J. (1993) 'Learning to teach and models of mentoring', in Kerry, I. and Shelton Mayes, A. (eds) (1995) *Issues in Mentoring*. London: Routledge/Open University.

McIntyre, D. and Hagger, H. (1996) *Mentors in Schools. Developing the profession of teaching*. London: David Fulton Publishers.

Montgomery, D. (1999) *Positive Teacher Appraisal Through Classroom Observation*. London: David Fulton Publishers.

Moyles, J. *et al.* (1999) 'Mentoring in primary schools: ethos, structures and workload', *Journal of In-service Education* **25**(1).

National Union of Teachers (NUT) (2000) *Managing Performance Management.* London: NUT.

OFSTED (1993) *Aspects of School Review in South Australia.* London: HMSO.

OFSTED (1998) *Inspection '98: Supplement to the inspection handbooks containing new requirements and guidance.* London: OFSTED Publications.

OFSTED (1999a) *Handbook for Inspecting Primary and Nursery Schools.* London: The Stationery Office.

OFSTED (1999b) *Raising the Attainment of Minority Ethnic Pupils – school and LEA responses.* London: OFSTED Publications Centre HMI 170.

OFSTED (2000a) *Annual Report of Her Majesty's Chief Inspector of Schools – Standards and quality in education 1998/99.* London: The Stationery Office.

OFSTED (2000b) *Improving City Schools.* London: OFSTED Publications Centre HMI 222.

OFSTED (2000c) *Evaluating Educational Inclusion – Guidance for inspectors and schools.* London: OFSTED Publications Centre HMI 235.

OFSTED (2000d) *Educational Inequality: Mapping race, class and gender.* OFSTED Publications Centre HM1 232.

OFSTED (2000e) *Improving City Schools: Strategies to promote educational improvement.* London: OFSTED Publications Centre HM1 222.

QCA (1999) *Keeping Track – Effective ways of recording pupil achievement to help raise standards.* London: QCA/99/382.

Richards, C. (2000) 'You don't have to be a genius, but . . .', Letter, *Times Educational Supplement,* 7 January.

Sisson, K. (ed.) (1995) *Personnel Management.* Oxford: Blackwell.

TTA (1999a) *Career Entry Profile.* London: TTA.

TTA (1999b) *Supporting Induction for Newly Qualified Teachers.* London: TTA.

TTA (2000) *Supporting Assessment for the Award of QTS.* London: TTA 102/2-00.

Thompson, M. (2000) 'Performance management – new wine in old bottles', *Professional Development Today* **3**(3).

Tower Hamlets Education Directorate (2000) *Starting Points: Guidance for assessment during the Foundation Stage.* London: LBTH Learning Design.

Tymms, P. (1999) *Baseline Assessment and Monitoring in Primary Schools: Achievements, attitudes and value-added indicators.* London: David Fulton Publishers.

Williams, A. and Prestage, S. (2000) *Still in at the Deep End? Developing strategies for the induction of new teachers.* London: Association of Teachers and Lecturers.

Winnacott, D. W. (1971) *Playing and Reality.* London: Tavistock.

Woods, P. and Jeffreys, B. (1996) *Teachable Moments. The art of teaching in primary schools.* Buckingham: Open University Press.

Wragg, E. C. *et al.* (1996) *Teacher Appraisal Observed.* London: Routledge.

Index